BOOK OF
ANIMALS

Kingfisher Books, Grisewood & Dempsey Ltd,
Elsley House, 24–30 Great Titchfield Street,
London W1P 7AD

First published in 1990 by Kingfisher Books
10 9 8 7 6 5 4
Copyright © Grisewood & Dempsey Ltd 1990

BRITISH LIBRARY CATALOGUING IN PUBLICATION DATA
Walters, Martin
    1. Animals
    I. Title
    591

ISBN 0 86272 464 3

Edited by Jacqui Bailey and Jackie Gaff
Picture research by Elaine Willis
Index by Trudi Braun and Peter Barber
Designed by David Jefferis and Janet King
Phototypeset by Southern Negatives and Positives (SPAN),
    Lingfield, Surrey
Printed in Spain

POCKET

BOOK OF

ANIMALS

MARTIN WALTERS

Kingfisher Books

Contents

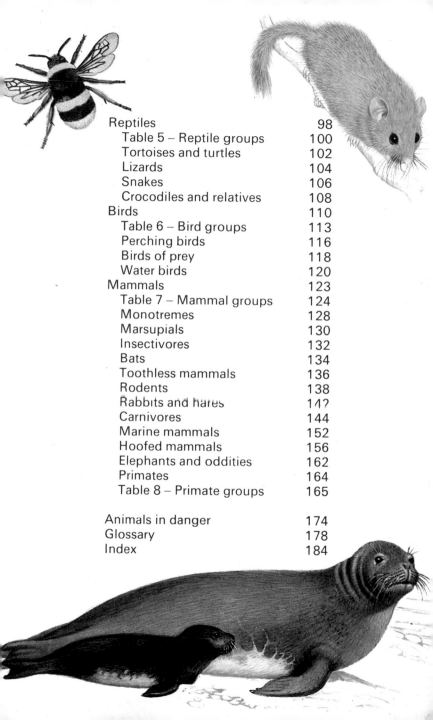

A Living Planet

The planet we live on is bursting with life. Indoors and outdoors, we are surrounded by hundreds of different animals and plants, in all shapes, colours and sizes. You only need to take a quick look around a garden or park in summer to discover a colourful range of flowers, trees and bushes, and many sorts of birds and insects. A trip to a zoo or a wildlife park reveals even more amazing variety – the animals of the deep oceans and the dry deserts, the wet forests and even the cold icy Arctic.

These are all things we can see with our eyes. Using a microscope opens up another world altogether – such as the hundreds of tiny water-fleas that swarm about in ponds or the insects called springtails which live in damp soil and leaf mould.

This book takes a look at the fascinating world of animals, from microscopic water-fleas to giants like the elephant and the Blue whale. The differences between the various animal types are explored, as well as the things they have in common. No matter how big they are or how small, all animals share certain characteristics – those that distinguish them from plants. The most important one is that animals catch and eat their food, moving around fairly actively so that they can do this. Plants, on the other hand, normally grow in one place for most of their lives, using the energy of the Sun to make their own food through photosynthesis.

▶ **Herds of zebra (family Equidae) and wildebeest (family Bovidae) browse side by side on the African plains. The chief enemy of both types of animal is the lion.**

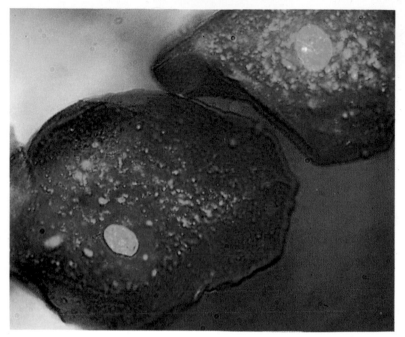

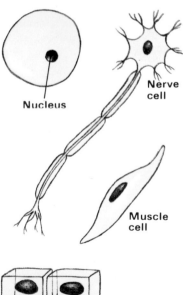

◀ ▲ **Cells come in all shapes** and are specialized to do different jobs. The human mouth cells in the photograph above have been magnified and stained blue.

Looking at life

The bodies of most living things are made up of tiny units called cells, each of which contains a special structure called a nucleus (plural nuclei). The nucleus acts as the cell's control centre, storing the instructions for making it grow and develop. A frog's egg is a cell, for example, and its nucleus tells it how to divide and grow into an adult. These instructions are passed on from generation to generation, each time an animal reproduces.

The bodies of the smallest animals in the world, the protozoans, are normally just a single cell with a nucleus. However, in their adult form, most other animals are made up of thousands or millions of cells, each with its own special job to do. Blood cells, nerve cells and muscle cells are just some of the different ones in human bodies.

Special scaffolding

The bigger an animal's body is, the more it needs a framework to hold it together and support its weight. In many animals, this framework is provided by a skeleton that includes a backbone. The bones that make up

▲ **A frog surrounded by its eggs, or spawn.** Each egg was a single cell when laid. Now the cells have multiplied and developed into tiny tadpoles.

the backbone are called vertebrae, and animals with backbones are known as vertebrates. This is not the largest grouping in the animal world, but it contains the biggest animals. Around 96 per cent of all animals are those without backbones, the invertebrates, such as flies and other insects, and worms.

Like the animal world, this book is divided into two main sections – the first one looks at the invertebrates, and the second at the vertebrates.

9

Animal records

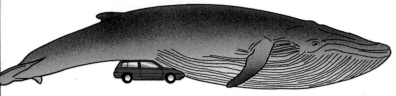

▲ **Largest** – at around 30 metres in length and weighing 135 tonnes, the Blue whale (*Balaenoptera musculus*) is the biggest animal that has ever lived. It is even bigger than the largest dinosaurs were.

▲ **Largest land animal** – the African elephant (*Loxodonta africana*) can weigh as much as 7 tonnes.

▼ **Tallest** – Giraffes (*Giraffa camelopardalis*) can be 5.5 metres tall and weigh up to 1 tonne.

▼ **Smallest vertebrate** – the Philippine goby (*Pandaka pygmaea*) grows to just 12 mm.

▶ **Smallest** – the invertebrate protozoans (phylum Protozoa) are often less than 0.01 mm in diameter.

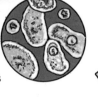

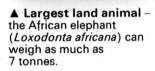

▼ **Longest** – Bootlace worms (*Lineus longissimus*) often grow to 30 metres, but sometimes reach 60 metres!

◀ **Longest lived** – Giant tortoises (genus *Geochelone*) have been recorded with lifespans of over 150 years.

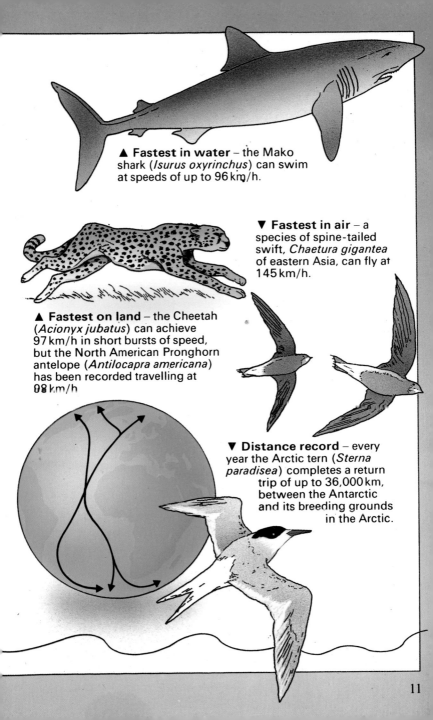

▲ **Fastest in water** – the Mako shark (*Isurus oxyrinchus*) can swim at speeds of up to 96 km/h.

▼ **Fastest in air** – a species of spine-tailed swift, *Chaetura gigantea* of eastern Asia, can fly at 145 km/h.

▲ **Fastest on land** – the Cheetah (*Acionyx jubatus*) can achieve 97 km/h in short bursts of speed, but the North American Pronghorn antelope (*Antilocapra americana*) has been recorded travelling at 98 km/h

▼ **Distance record** – every year the Arctic tern (*Sterna paradisea*) completes a return trip of up to 36,000 km, between the Antarctic and its breeding grounds in the Arctic.

11

Grouping Living Things

Nearly 1.3 million different animals have been identified and named by biologists. This is just the tip of a vast living iceberg, however, and the total number is probably closer to 5 million! Because of this enormous variety biologists have developed a special system of naming living things. This system classifies things at the same time, by grouping together those that share similar features.

Individual animals and plants are identified by a special double name, called a binomial. The binomial is always in Latin form and is written in italic script. The African elephant, for example, is *Loxodonta africana*. Often the names describe some aspect of the animal or plant – *Loxodonta* means 'slanting tooth' and describes the elephant's long curved tusks.

The classification system

The modern classification system has seven major ranks, or levels – species, genus (plural genera), family, order, class, phylum (plural phyla) and kingdom. The species name is the second part of the binomial and is unique to the particular animal or plant. Related species are grouped into the same genus. As an example, the binomial for the Domestic dog is *Canis familiaris*. *Canis*, which means 'dog' in Latin, is the genus name, and *familiaris* is the species name.

Wolves are closely related to the Domestic dog, so they belong to the same genus, *Canis*. The Grey wolf is *Canis lupus*, for example.

The next stage in the classification pyramid is the family name. The Grey wolf and the Domestic dog both belong to the family Canidae. Other members of this family are the Indian fox (*Vulpes bengalensis*) and the Fennec fox (*Vulpes zerda*) – their genus is *Vulpes*, not *Canis*.

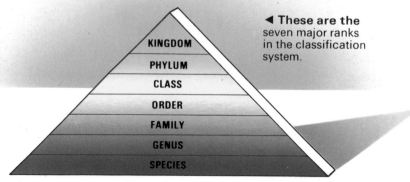

◀ These are the seven major ranks in the classification system.

KINGDOM
PHYLUM
CLASS
ORDER
FAMILY
GENUS
SPECIES

The classification of the Fennec fox of North Africa is:

Kingdom: Animalia
  Phylum: Chordata
    Class: Mammalia
    Order: Carnivora
    Family: Canidae
    Genus: *Vulpes*
    Species: *zerda*

Climbing the ladder

The order name is the next step up the pyramid. The family Canidae belongs to the order Carnivora, which means 'meat-eating'. Among the other members of this order are the cats (family Felidae) and the bears (family Ursidae).

Then comes the class name. The order Carnivora is just one of 20 orders in the class Mammalia, the mammals. These are animals that feed their young on milk – humans (order Primates) are also members of the class Mammalia.

Together with other animals that have backbones, such as birds (class Aves) and reptiles (class Reptilia), mammals are grouped in the phylum Chordata. The phyla are almost at the top of the classification pyramid. Beyond them are four kingdoms – plants, animals, bacteria, and fungi and relatives (the last two are discussed on page 15).

The classification system used in this book recognizes 33 phyla in the animal kingdom, and these are set out in table 1 on page 17. Comparing the approximate number of species identified in each phylum will show you how greatly they vary, with the Arthropoda (joint-limbed animals) containing by far the most.

The classification of Jackson's chameleon of East Africa is:

Kingdom: Animalia
  Phylum: Chordata
    Class: Reptilia
    Order: Squamata
    Family: Chamaeleontidae
    Genus: *Chamaeleo*
    Species: *jacksoni*

How animals are grouped

Classification is based upon comparing living things and seeing how many features they share. All animals have a similar set of problems to deal with in their lives, such as how to move, how to breathe, and how to feed. Most animals are grouped according to similarities in the ways in which their bodies are designed to deal with one or more of these problems. Thus the meat-eating animals such as cats and dogs in the order Carnivora all share the same type of jaw and teeth.

Sometimes animals that live in similar environments or share a particular lifestyle are classified in different groups. Birds and bats can both fly and they have well-developed wings, but birds belong to the class Aves and bats to the class Mammalia. Unlike birds, whose bodies are covered by feathers, bats have fur and, like all mammals, they feed their young on milk. Whales are mammals for the same reason, even though their watery habitat and streamlined bodies are things they share with the fish classes.

These variations arise because it isn't just the outside shape of an animal which biologists take into consideration during classification, but also its internal organs (especially the skeleton and bones), and even the stages in its development from egg to adult. Thus the snakes, lizards and other animals in the class Reptilia all lay large leathery eggs, are cold-blooded, and breathe through lungs. Members of the class Amphibia such as frogs, on the other hand, are also cold-blooded, but they lay jelly-like eggs which become tadpoles. And although some amphibians have lungs and breathe air, others breathe through their skin or through organs called gills which are able to absorb oxygen from water.

Living kingdoms

Two other kingdoms are recognized by biologists for classification purposes, apart from the

▼ **Cells of the bacterium** *Bacillus subtilis*, which causes eye infections in humans. The photograph was taken through a microscope and dyed to show the parts of the cells clearly – the nuclei are orange.

plant and animal kingdoms. The kingdom Monera is where bacteria (singular bacterium) are grouped. These are microscopic organisms – the biggest is a fraction of a millimetre – whose cells do not have a nucleus. About 5000 species of bacteria have been identified, compared with around 350,000 species of plants and 1.3 million animals.

The other major grouping is the kingdom Fungi, which contains around 44,000 species of mushrooms, toadstools and moulds. Unlike plants, which are usually green and make their own food internally through photosynthesis, fungi (singular

▲ **Ink-caps (genus *Coprinus*)** are a type of mushroom, classified in the kingdom Fungi.

fungus) digest food which is outside their bodies, absorbing it through their cell walls.

Finally, there is one last group of living things which do not fit into the classification system at all. Viruses do not have cells of their own, and they can only survive inside another living organism, be it a bacterium, a fungus, a plant or an animal. Viruses often cause disease. In humans, for example, different viruses are responsible for colds, chickenpox, measles and mumps.

▲ **Butterflies (class Insecta)** are members of the phylum Arthropoda – with nearly 1 million species, this is by far the largest of the animal phyla.

The butterfly above is a Monarch (*Danaus plexippus*). It is found throughout the Americas and has spread across the Pacific to South-East Asia.

Table 1 – Animal phyla

Phylum	Common name	Species known*
Protozoa	Protozoans	35,000
Placozoa	Placozoans	2
Porifera	Sponges	10,000
Coelenterata/Cnidaria	Jellyfish & relatives	10,000
Ctenophora	Sea gooseberries	100
Platyhelminthes	Flatworms & relatives	25,000
Mesozoa	Mesozoans	50
Gnathostomula	Gnathostomulans	100
Nemertea	Proboscis worms/Nemertines	900
Gastrotricha	Gastrotrichs	450
Rotifera	Wheel animals	1800
Kinorhyncha	Kinorhynchs	100
Priapula	Priapulans/Priapulid worms	10
Acanthocephala	Thorny/Spiny-headed worms	1000
Nematoda	Roundworms	15,000
Nematomorpha	Horsehair/Gordian worms	250
Sipuncula	Peanut worms	350
Echiura	Spoon worms	150
Pogonophora	Beard worms	100
Annelida	Segmented/Ringed worms	15,000
Mollusca	Molluscs	99,000
Phorona	Horseshoe worms	10
Brachiopoda	Lamp shells	350
Bryozoa/Ectoprocta/Polyzoa	Moss animals	4000
Entoprocta	Entoprocts	150
Arthropoda	Arthropods	1,000,000
Onychophora	Velvet worms	120
Tardigrada	Water bears	400
Pentastoma	Tongue worms	100
Chaetognatha	Arrow worms	70
Hemichordata	Acorn worms & relatives	100
Echinodermata	Starfish & relatives	6250
Chordata**	Chordates	46,400
Subphylum Urochordata	Sea squirts & relatives	*1400*
Subphylum Cephalochordata	Lancelets	*25*
Subphylum Vertebrata	Vertebrates	*45,000*

*Rounded totals.
**The phylum Chordata is divided into three groups called subphyla. One of these, subphylum Vertebrata, contains all of the animals with backbones.

Using This Book

There are so many different species of animal that it is only possible to explore the main phyla in this book. The first section looks at the largest of the invertebrate phyla. It starts with the simplest animals, the protozoans, and works through roughly in order of increasing complexity. The phylum Arthropoda is so large (see table 2, on pages 46–47) that it has been broken down into some of its classes and the orders within them.

Most of the book is given over to the bigger and more familiar animals, the vertebrates. These are explored in greater detail, class by class, starting with fish and ending with mammals. Six more tables are distributed through the section. Like the first two tables these list various animals' ranks, giving scientific and common names, as well as the number of species now identified.

Phylum **PROTOZOA** – Single-celled animals

Phylum **PORIFERA** – Sponges

Phylum **COELENTERATA** – Jellyfish & relatives

Phylum **PLATYHELMINTHES** – Flatworms & relatives

Phylum **ROTIFERA** – Wheel animals

Phylum **NEMATODA** – Roundworms

Phylum **ANNELIDA** – Segmented worms

Phylum **MOLLUSCA** – Molluscs

Phylum **ARTHROPODA** – Joint-limbed animals

Phylum **TARDIGRADA** – Water bears

Phylum **ECHINODERMATA** – Starfish & relatives

Phylum **CHORDATA** – Chordates

Whenever a particular animal species is mentioned in this book, its common name is highlighted by capitalizing the first letter – the Grey wolf, for example, or the Blue whale. The binomial (genus and species names) is always given in italic script.

A glossary at the back of the book explains some of the new or difficult words you may come across. You'll also find that the shared characteristics of each major grouping – phylum, class or order – have been highlighted throughout the book to provide an easy reference tool. These classification summaries are in pale yellow boxes. Comparing the information in the different boxes will enable you to identify at a glance the features that distinguish one animal group from another.

A final chapter briefly examines some of the threats to the survival of the rarer species of animal, and considers what can be done to preserve them and their habitats. Species that are allowed to become extinct can never be replaced – this is the tragedy of the marvellous world of animal life with which we share the Earth.

These are the major animal phyla discussed in this book. As the table on page 17 shows, most animals are invertebrates.

Invertebrates

Vertebrates

Class MAMMALIA – Mammals

Class AVES – Birds

Class REPTILIA – Snakes & relatives

Class AMPHIBIA – Frogs & relatives

Class OSTEICHTHYES – Bony fish

Class CHONDRICHTHYES – Cartilaginous fish

Class AGNATHA – Jawless fish

Subphylum VERTEBRATA – Vertebrates

Subphylum UROCHORDATA – Sea squirts & relatives

Subphylum CEPHALOCHORDATA – Lancelets

Invertebrates

Invertebrates are animals without backbones, and they account for about 96 per cent of all animal species. Many are very small and not easily spotted, but they can be found in almost every habitat imaginable – in forests and grasslands, in gardens and deserts, in fresh and salt water, rivers and seas. Many species live in water, in fact, and the insects and the arachnids (spiders and relatives) are the only major groups within the invertebrates to have mastered the art of survival on dry land.

Other invertebrates include jellyfish, shrimps, crabs and starfish – they are as varied as their habitats. In size, they range from the tiny protozoans, which can only be seen under a microscope, to the 20-metre bulk of the Giant squid (*Architeuthis dux*)!

Although they lack the vertebrates' bony internal skeleton, invertebrates show a wide spectrum of body shape and structure. Most protozoans, jellyfish and worms have soft bodies. The bodies of some species, including many of the worms, are supported by the pressure of the fluid inside them. Other invertebrates are supported externally, by the water in which they live.

The bodies of many invertebrates have stronger support and protection. Snails have shells, for example, while insects and spiders have a tough exterior 'skin' called an exoskeleton.

▶ **Insects like this Acorn** weevil (*Balaminus venosus*) are invertebrates – unlike vertebrates, they do not have a bony internal skeleton and a backbone. Instead, insect bodies are supported and strengthened by a tough 'skin' called an exoskeleton.

Protozoans

Unlike all other animals, which are made up of large numbers of cells, typical protozoans are just a single cell with a nucleus, lacking in obvious body parts like a head, gut or tail. Some scientists think that the protozoans' simple body structure makes them similar to that of the earliest forms of life on Earth. In fact, the word protozoan means 'first animal'.

Many species of Protozoa have a very simple method of reproducing – they split in two. First the nucleus divides and then the whole animal splits in half, to make two similar but separate individuals. Each individual may divide two or three times every day. This kind of rapid reproduction allows protozoan populations to increase very quickly when the conditions are suitable and food is plentiful.

There are around 35,000 species in the phylum, most of them visible only with the help of a microscope. The biggest protozoans reach 0.1 mm, however, and can just be seen with the naked eye.

You can grow protozoans at home by putting damp soil or pond mud into a jar of water and adding a little chopped up hay. Place the jar in a light place, but not in direct sunshine, and leave it for several

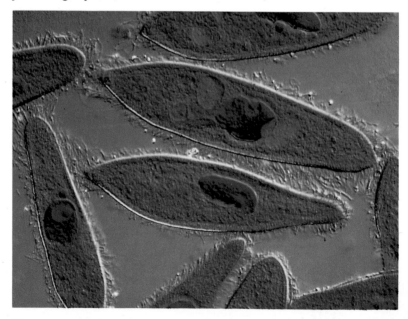

days. The mixture should turn into a rich protozoan 'soup', but you'll have to use a lens or microscope to see individual creatures.

Moving and multiplying

Some protozoans, such as amoebae (singular amoeba), can change shape by moving the fluid inside their bodies around. They get about in the same way, flowing into temporary leg-like growths. These outgrowths are called pseudopodia (singular pseudopodium), which means 'false legs'. Amoebae also use their pseudopodia to catch food particles as they glide along, flowing around the food and engulfing it.

Other protozoans have different ways of moving. Members of the genus *Euglena* have a special hair-like growth called a flagellum which they use to whip themselves along. *Paramecium* species are covered in smaller 'hairs' called cilia (singular cilium), which beat constantly to create a rippling movement.

Protozoans are the most numerous animals alive, with enormous quantities of the various species existing in a wide range of habitats. Many spend their lives feeding and reproducing on the cells of other animals. An organism that lives and feeds on the body of another species is called a parasite, and the animal on which it lives is called the host. Many parasitic protozoans cause diseases that infect their host animals. Malaria and sleeping sickness are two such diseases.

◄ *Paramecium* species move by beating tiny hair-like cilia, visible here surrounding each animal's body like a fringe.

▶ *Amoeba* (above) is a protozoan which moves by flowing out into leg-like growths called pseudopodia. *Euglena* (below) whips itself along through the water with its long tail-like flagellum.

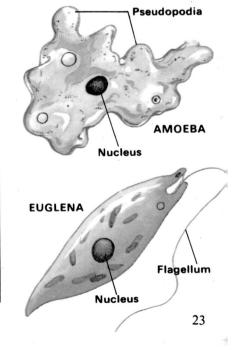

Pseudopodia

AMOEBA

Nucleus

EUGLENA

Flagellum

Nucleus

Phylum Protozoa

- Body not divided into cells
- Majority invisible to naked eye; some grow to pinhead size
- Move by flowing, waving flagella, or beating cilia
- Almost all aquatic

23

Sponges

One of the main differences between plants and animals is that plants tend to spend their lives fixed in one place, whereas animals are able to move about. There are exceptions to most rules, however, and sponges are unusual among animals in that as adults they remain firmly attached in one place. At first glance, sponges seem to live in a rather plant-like way, rooted to rocks, coral or seaweed. At one time, even scientists thought sponges were plants. It wasn't until they were examined in detail, with the help of microscopes, that sponges were classified as animals.

The name of the sponge phylum, Porifera, means 'hole-carrying', and sponge bodies are full of holes through which water constantly flows. Sponges live on food particles carried with the water. They are basically very efficient living water filters, so they do not need to move about in search of food.

You may have noticed natural bath sponges on sale in shops, or have one yourself. These bath sponges are actually the soft skeletons of species such as *Spongia officinalis*, which is common in the Mediterranean Sea. Similar species are found in the Caribbean Sea and are also harvested for their soft skeletons.

A living sponge has a soft fleshy body which is supported by a harder skeleton. Not all sponge skeletons are as soft as those of the bath sponges, and some species have very hard spiky skeletons.

Most of the 10,000 or so sponge species live in the sea, although a few are found in fresh water. They come in all shapes and sizes. Some are shaped like cups or vases, but others are round and tube-like, or flattened, or even finely branched like the twigs on a tree.

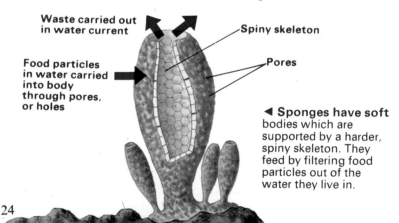

Waste carried out in water current

Spiny skeleton

Food particles in water carried into body through pores, or holes

Pores

◄ Sponges have soft bodies which are supported by a harder, spiny skeleton. They feed by filtering food particles out of the water they live in.

Phylum Porifera

- Skeleton of spiky fibres
- Body full of holes, through which water flows; feed by filtering this water
- Mobile only before adult stage
- All aquatic; mostly marine

▶ **The skeleton of a Venus'** flower basket sponge (genus *Euplectella*).

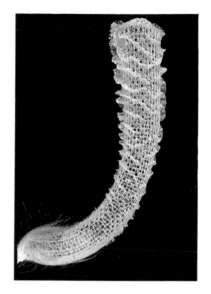

▼ **A variety of sponge species** growing side by side, in the warm waters of the Caribbean Sea. The pores through which food-bearing water enters a sponge show clearly in the red species.

Jellyfish and Relatives

Jellyfish, sea-anemones, hydras and corals are all related, as members of the phylum Coelenterata. Like many animals, they get their name from a description of their bodies. Coelenterates have a single body opening which leads into a hollow gut – coel means 'hollow' and enteron means 'gut'. Their body plan is circular, and the gut opening is surrounded by tentacles, as the illustration below shows. Coelenterates have soft bodies and consist of two layers of cells sandwiching a jelly-like substance. In many species this jelly layer is thin, but in jellyfish it is very thick and fills most of the body.

Sea-anemones and hydras

With their 'heads' of waving, petal-like tentacles, sea-anemones (class Anthozoa) look very like underwater flowers. They appear to be firmly attached to the rocks on which they sit, but they do move about and can change position by gliding slowly along – sometimes they bend over and somersault to a new spot! Sea-anemones change shape when the tide goes out, shrivelling up into a blob until the water returns.

Hydras (class Hydrozoa) are a bit like elongated sea-anemones with long waving tentacles. They are quite common in fresh water, where they can be found clinging to plants and feeding on any small water animals that happen to blunder into their arms.

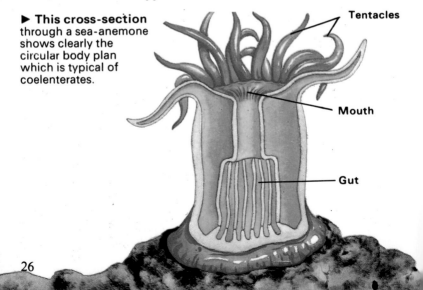

▶ **This cross-section** through a sea-anemone shows clearly the circular body plan which is typical of coelenterates.

Tentacles

Mouth

Gut

▲ **The delicately coloured** sea-anemone *Sagartia elegans* occurs in the North Sea.

▶ **Hydras are small (about** 1 cm long) freshwater relatives of sea-anemones and jellyfish.

Phylum Coelenterata
- Circular body, with single opening surrounded by tentacles
- Soft-bodied
- Sandwich-like body wall (two layers with jelly between)
- Aquatic; nearly all marine

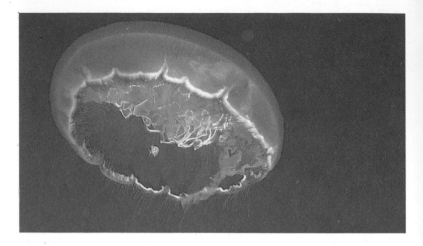

Jellyfish

A jellyfish is rather like an upside-down hydra or sea-anemone, with its tentacles hanging beneath it. It has the same two-layered body, but the jelly in the 'sandwich' is much thicker and takes up most of its body. Jellyfish move about more freely than other coelenterates.

You may have come across jellyfish at the seaside, washed up on the beach as lifeless blobs. Alive and in water, they take on a different appearance altogether. They are among the most graceful sights of the marine world, drifting slowly along by opening and closing their bodies like umbrellas, with their tentacles trailing beneath them.

There are two different kinds of jellyfish. Some, like the Common jellyfish (*Aurelia aurita*), are individuals – each one is a single animal. These jellyfish are grouped in the class Scyphozoa.

Other jellyfish species are not what they appear. They may look like a single animal, but they are actually made up of a whole colony of individuals. Colonial species are grouped in the class Hydrozoa, with the hydras, and they include the venomous Portuguese man-o'-war (genus *Physalia*) shown opposite.

The individuals that make up colonial jellyfish behave a bit like the separate cells in more usual animals. Each is specialized to do a particular job, such as feeding or providing movement.

Stun-gun tentacles

Most jellyfish feed by catching fish, shrimps and other animals in their tentacles as they drift about near the surface of the sea. They paralyze their prey with venom from special cell structures called nematocysts. The food is then moved into the mouth and on into the gut where

◀ **This jellyfish is a** single animal, unlike the colonial Portuguese man-o'-war to the right. Its mouth is in the centre underneath its body, surrounded by arms. Jellyfish like this move by opening and closing their whole body, rather like an umbrella furling and unfurling.

▶ **The Portuguese** man-o'-war (the species shown here is *Physalia utriculis*) is a colonial animal. It is made up of different types of individual jellyfish, each one specialized to do a particular job – some are for stinging, others are for feeding or reproducing.

it is broken down and digested.

Nematocysts are a weapon common to all coelenterates, and in most species they are part of the skin cells covering the tentacles. Each nematocyst has a hair-like trigger which releases a poison dart when the coelenterate's prey brushes against it. Other special cell structures send out sticky threads which help to entangle the stunned prey in the animal's tentacles. Nematocysts have made the slow-moving coelenterates very efficient at catching even speedy swimmers like shrimps and fish.

COELENTERATE RECORDS

Largest – the jellyfish species *Cyanea arctica* can grow to 3.6 metres in diameter and have tentacles 36 metres long. With 12-metre-long tentacles, Portuguese men-o'-war are also huge.

Most dangerous – people have died from the venomous stings of the sea wasps *Chironex fleckeri* and *Chiropsalmus quadrigatus*, found in tropical waters off South-East Asia.

Corals and reefs

Some corals live as individuals, but many are colonial animals made up of separate units called polyps. The polyps in colonial species are connected together by a thin layer of tissue.

When they are alive, individual coral polyps look like tiny sea-anemones. More familiar, perhaps, are the brittle, rock-like skeletons corals leave behind them when they die. In some species, the skeletons build up into the coral masses called reefs. These reef-building species are colonial, and the polyps' chalk-like skeletons take thousands of years to build into a reef.

The world's biggest coral reef is the Great Barrier Reef, which is over 2000 kilometres long and lies off the tropical north-east coast of Australia. Corals can only grow well in sea water that is clean, warm and fairly shallow, and they are very often found around tropical islands.

Corals usually feed at night, the polyps spreading out their tentacles to trap tiny animals floating past in the sea water. However, some scientists think corals also have another method of feeding. Their bodies have been found to contain microscopic plants, which make food from the energy of the Sun through photosynthesis. These plant 'guests' may also give out chemicals which help the corals to make their chalky skeletons. Both theories might explain why corals can only thrive in shallow water, where sunlight can easily filter through to them.

◄ **Reefs are rich in** animal life, the corals providing many species with protection from the waves and safe places to hide from predators. Here, a shoal of fish weaves in and out of Red Sea coral.

► **A live reef-building** coral, *Tubastraea coccinea*, photographed in close-up. Two of the polyps have opened, spreading their tentacles to feed.

Worms

If you look at the table on page 17, you'll see that the animal kingdom contains many phyla with the word 'worm' in their common name. Most are not true worm phyla, however. There are three major types of true worm – flatworms and relatives (phylum Platyhelminthes), roundworms (phylum Nematoda), and segmented worms (phylum Annelida). They are all soft animals with long bodies suitable for a burrowing lifestyle. As you would expect from their names, flatworms have a flattened body plan, while roundworms are more or less round in cross-section, and segmented worms are tube-shaped and clearly marked in sections.

Flatworms

Some flatworm species are parasites which live and feed inside other animals, including humans. These parasites include flukes and tapeworms, which are both major causes of disease, especially in tropical regions.

Flukes (class Trematoda) live as parasites inside the bodies of vertebrates. Some species live in the lungs, for example, or in the liver or the intestine. Flukes cause diseases in domestic animals such as cows and sheep, as well as in people.

Tapeworms (class Cestoda) live as parasites inside the intestines of vertebrates, fastening themselves on with the suckers and hooks on their heads. They are ribbon shaped and grow by forming new sections just behind the head.

Other flatworms live freely and are not parasites, however. These are grouped in the class Turbellaria. Different species are common in the sea, as well as in streams and ponds. They glide slowly over weeds and rocks, partly guided by simple light-sensitive eyespots on their heads. These eyespots can only detect light. They cannot see objects in the way human eyes can. A flatworm won't usually move into a bright light, preferring to turn away in search of the dark where it is better hidden from its enemies. It's usually possible to find flatworms if you search underneath stones in streams.

Some flatworm species have an amazing ability to reproduce by splitting. If one of them is cut into sections, each piece will regrow the missing part and become a new, complete individual. These species can also feed on their own bodies if food is short. They get smaller and smaller as they digest themselves, starting to grow again when food becomes available once more.

► **Flatworms have** thin bodies and are often leaf-shaped, like this candy-striped species, *Prostheceraeus vittatus*, from the Atlantic Ocean. This flatworm grows to about 3 cm and bears two tentacles on its head.

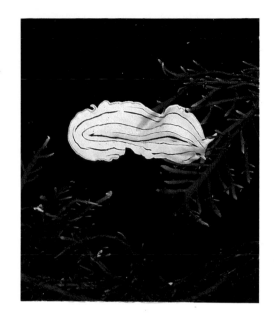

Roundworms

These are the most numerous of the many-celled animals. Some people estimate that fertile soils may contain over 10 million roundworms within 1 square metre! They live in an amazing variety of damp habitats. One species (*Turbatrix aceti*) even lives in old vinegar!

Like flatworms, some roundworms are parasitic, while others are free-living. Several kinds of parasitic roundworm cause disease in animals, including humans. One of the most severe is caused by the hookworm (genus *Ancylostoma*), which lives in the gut. Hookworm disease is very widespread, particularly in tropical countries – around 9 per cent of the world's population are thought to suffer from it.

Other roundworms are parasitic on plants. The Potato root eelworm (*Globodera rostochiensis*) eats into potatoes while they are still attached to the living plant, for example. It is a major pest of potato crops.

Phylum Nematoda

- Non-segmented worms
- Rounded body, tapering at both ends
- Known in all habitats

Phylum Platyhelminthes

- Non-segmented worms
- Soft-bodied and flat, with recognizable head and tail
- Body can regrow after injury
- Found in water or damp places

Segmented worms

This phylum, Annelida, contains the earthworms that are so common in gardens and fields, as well as leeches and a wide range of bristleworms. With around 15,000 species, it is the largest worm phylum. All members have bodies that are divided into similar, repeating segments.

You've probably seen birds running across a lawn in the morning, searching for earthworms. These worms (class Oligochaeta) spend most of their lives underground, feeding as they burrow, by swallowing the soil and digesting the decaying leaves and other food material in it. The rest is excreted as wormcasts on the surface of the soil.

Many leech species (class Hirudinea) feed by sucking the blood of other animals, usually mammals or fish. They attach themselves to their prey with suckers and use their saw-like teeth to drill a hole. Before sucking out the blood, leeches inject a special chemical which stops the blood from clotting. This allows the blood to flow freely into the leech's body. A leech swells to several times its normal size during a feed. Afterwards it drops off again, and can survive for months before the next meal.

Sea worms

Bristleworms (class Polychaeta) are nearly all marine. They include lugworms, whose casts you may have seen on sandy beaches.

At first glance another marine group in this class, the fanworms, look more like plants than segmented worms. Like sponges, fanworms live permanently attached to the seabed, or to rocks or shells. They use their feather-like tentacles to filter food particles from the water.

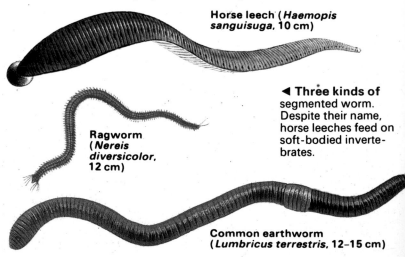

Horse leech (*Haemopis sanguisuga*, 10 cm)

◄ Three kinds of segmented worm. Despite their name, horse leeches feed on soft-bodied invertebrates.

Ragworm (*Nereis diversicolor*, 12 cm)

Common earthworm (*Lumbricus terrestris*, 12–15 cm)

▲ **A feather-duster fanworm** from the coral reefs of Mauritius, in the Indian Ocean.

▶ **The sea-mouse (genus** *Aphrodite*) is a flattened marine bristleworm which creeps along the seabed. Its covering of shiny bristles makes it look more like a mouse than a worm.

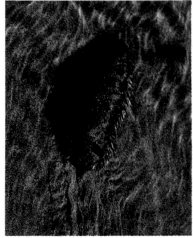

Phylum Annelida

- Segmented worms
- Tubular body
- Most have bristles, but leeches have suckers
- Terrestrial or aquatic

Wheel Animals and Water Bears

These two unusual animal phyla are not related, but they share an adaptation to a difficult habitat. They both live in watery places that regularly dry out, and they have remarkable ways of surviving periods of drought.

Wheel animals (phylum Rotifera) are among the smallest of many-celled creatures. The largest species grow to 3 mm, but many are microscopic, like the protozoans. The word rotifera means 'wheel-carrying', and the name comes from the wheel-like structures on the animals' heads. These 'wheels' are actually rings of tiny hair-like cilia. The cilia beat in a regular rhythm and make a current of water to draw in food particles, as well as propelling the animal through the water.

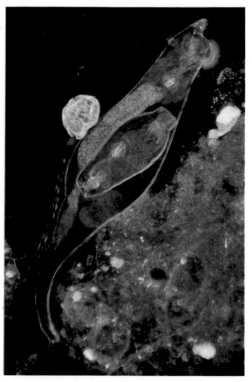

◄ **Wheel animals** take their name from the rings of hair-like cilia on their heads. Since they are small and often transparent, they are seen best under a microscope. The young of the wheel animal shown here (genus *Rotaria*) can be seen inside its body.

► **Water bears feed** on pond vegetation, clambering about on their four pairs of stumpy legs. Each leg has sharp claws at the tip, which help the animal to grip. This red species belongs to the genus *Hypsibius*.

When the water they live in dries out, wheel animals go into a state of 'living death', drying out completely and only 'coming alive' again when the water returns. They can stay 'dead' in this dry state for many years, and survive temperatures as low as –200°C through to the heat of 40°C!

There are about 1800 species of wheel animal, and they are found in birdbaths and rainwater guttering, as well as in seasonal pools of water. The pink colour that birdbaths sometimes have is often caused by a red species. You could try growing some wheel animals yourself by collecting caked greenish-coloured mud from a dried-out pool and putting it in water. The wheel animals should appear within an hour, but you'll need a microscope to see them.

Water bears (phylum Tardigrada) can also shrivel up and go into a type of 'living death' when their watery homes dry out, surviving like this for as long as 60 years. They are found on water plants in ponds, as well as on mosses and in damp soils. There are around 400 species but, once again, you'll need a microscope to see them properly.

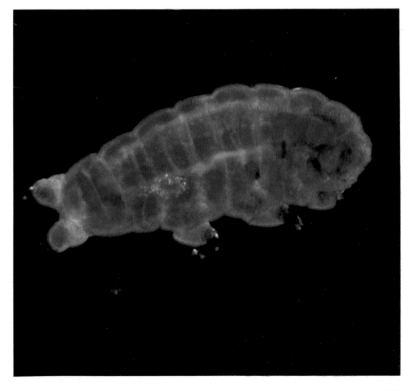

Molluscs

This is one of the most varied of the animal phyla. It embraces slugs and snails, oysters, clams and other shelled sea creatures, as well as octopuses and their relatives.

Many molluscs have a hard shell on their backs, to protect their soft bodies from attack by other animals. Some molluscs – snails, for example – have a single shell, while others have two shells which are hinged together. Most single-shelled molluscs are grouped in the class Gastropoda and called gastropods. There are around 77,000 species. However the class Gastropoda also includes animals that don't have an obvious shell – slugs, for example. There are 20,000 or so species of double-shelled molluscs, or bivalves, grouped in the class Bivalvia.

Octopuses, cuttlefish and squid belong to the class Cephalopoda, which contains about 650 species. Few members of this class have an obvious shell, but squid and cuttlefish have a shell-like bone inside them. People often buy these cuttlebones to give to pet birds, to provide calcium and for beak sharpening.

Mollusc features

As you can see in the diagrams opposite, gastropods and bivalves both have some form of soft muscular foot. Gastropods crawl around on theirs – the word gastro-pod actually means 'stomach-foot'.

An attribute that gastropods and cephalopods share is a head that carries tentacles and eyes. Most molluscs also have a rasping tongue called a radula, which is set with tiny teeth-like pegs. It works rather like a file, rubbing food from plants and rocks.

◄ **The enlarged surface of a** mollusc's radula, or tongue. Its rows of rough teeth-like pegs work as a file, rasping food from plants and rocks.

Phylum Mollusca

- Most have shells (sometimes inside body)
- Mouth with radula (rasping tongue)
- Muscular foot
- Terrestrial or aquatic (freshwater and marine)

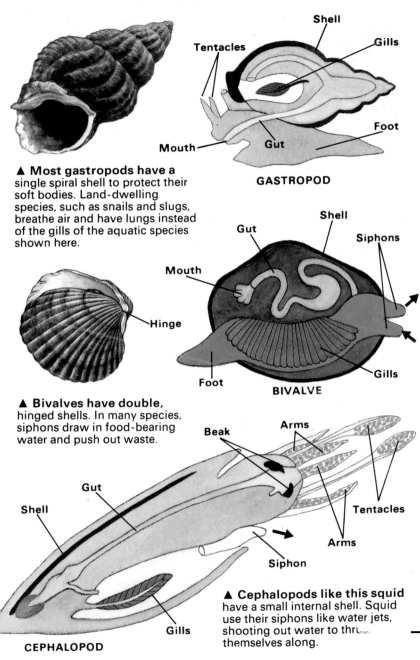

GASTROPOD

▲ **Most gastropods have a** single spiral shell to protect their soft bodies. Land-dwelling species, such as snails and slugs, breathe air and have lungs instead of the gills of the aquatic species shown here.

Labels: Tentacles, Shell, Gills, Mouth, Gut, Foot

BIVALVE

▲ **Bivalves have double,** hinged shells. In many species, siphons draw in food-bearing water and push out waste.

Labels: Hinge, Gut, Mouth, Shell, Siphons, Foot, Gills

CEPHALOPOD

▲ **Cephalopods like this squid** have a small internal shell. Squid use their siphons like water jets, shooting out water to thru... themselves along.

Labels: Beak, Arms, Gut, Shell, Tentacles, Arms, Siphon, Gills

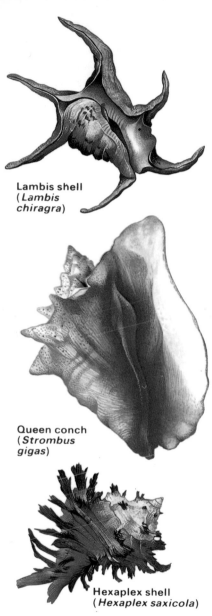

Lambis shell
(*Lambis
chiragra*)

Queen conch
(*Strombus
gigas*)

Hexaplex shell
(*Hexaplex saxicola*)

▲ **Some of the beautifully**
coloured shells of gastropods that
inhabit tropical waters.

Sea shells

The marine gastropods show a beautiful range of differently shaped and patterned shells. Among the most attractive and highly prized are those of a type of sea snail, the cone shells (genus *Conus*). The delicately coloured and patterned shells of these animals range in size from about 5 to 20 cm long.

In life, cone shell snails are dangerous. Their radulas, or rasping tongues, are set with hollow teeth which can inject a powerful poison. The poison is usually employed to paralyze worms and other live food, which is then eaten. Even so, cone shells do sting if attacked or disturbed in any way, and the poison of some species is deadly to humans.

Many less exotic and more familiar seaside molluscs are bivalves, including cockles, mussels, oysters, clams and scallops. Among the marine bivalve species is the Pearl mussel (*Pinctada martensii*), which as its name suggests is the source of the natural pearls used in jewellery.

Most bivalves feed by pulling in a current of water and filtering out anything edible. Some species draw the water in through a special tube called a siphon, passing the water out afterwards through another tube. Bivalves can feed without opening their hinged shells very far, and they are quite capable of 'clamming up' again with great speed if something disturbs them.

The scallop (genus *Pecten*) can swim using its shell. If attacked, it repeatedly opens and shuts its shell, squirting out a rapid water jet which shoots it jerkily along the seabed.

Burrowing is a speciality of some bivalves. Many use their foot to dig themselves into sand or mud. The foot pushes out and down, then drags the shell after it. Bivalves like the shipworm (genus *Teredo*) dig into wood, causing damage to piers and the hulls of ships and boats. Piddocks (genera *Pholas* and *Zirphaea*) are bivalves that grind away with their shells to bore holes into clay or soft rock. It takes a piddock about two hours to burrow 1 mm into soft rock such as limestone.

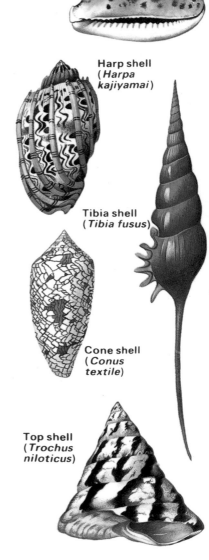

Tiger cowrie
(*Cypraea tigris*)

Harp shell
(*Harpa kajiyamai*)

Tibia shell
(*Tibia fusus*)

Cone shell
(*Conus textile*)

Top shell
(*Trochus niloticus*)

▲ **Many marine gastropods** are threatened with extinction, because their shells are collect▸

MOLLUSC RECORDS

Largest – the Giant squid (*Architeuthis dux*) can be 20 metres long from its 'tail' to the tip of its tentacles.

Smallest – some of the members of the worm-like class Neomeniomorpha are just 1 mm long.

Largest bivalve – Giant clams (*Tridacna derasa*) can weigh more than 225 kg and be 1.2 metres across.

Heaviest land mollusc – the African giant snail (*Achatina fulica*) can be 20 cm long and weigh as much as 1.1 kg!

Cephalopods

This mollusc class contains the largest and most intelligent of the invertebrate animals. Octopuses (order Octopoda) have particularly large brains, which are part of their well-developed nervous system. They can even be trained to tell the difference between simple shapes, such as a cross and a square – quite an achievement for a relative of the humble garden slug!

The other members of this class, squid and cuttlefish, are grouped in the order Decapoda. The word decapoda means 'ten feet', and squid and cuttlefish have eight arms and two, longer tentacles. Octopuses have eight arms of similar length – their order name means 'eight feet'.

▲ **A Lesser or Curled octopus** (*Eledone cirrhosa*) clings to the rocks with its tentacles.

Cephalopods' arms and tentacles all have suction pads which are used to help capture prey. Octopuses also use their arms to help them to clamber along underwater – they rarely swim.

As well as the typical mollusc radula, cephalopods have a pair of hard sharp jaws, known as the beak. This they use to tear up their food – mostly crustaceans and fish.

All cephalopods seem to have good eyesight and can focus clearly upon objects. They have a pair of large eyes, one on either side of the head. The mournful eyes of the octopus are particularly remarkable.

Cephalopods' eyes look very much like those of vertebrate animals, but they actually work in a very different way. Vertebrates focus by changing the shape of the lens in their eyes, but in an octopus' eyes it is the distance between the retina at the back of the eyeball and the lens that changes.

Squid and cuttlefish

Most squid are larger than cuttlefish and many species are adapted for swimming in the open sea. These squid species are streamlined in shape and have a triangular body-fin which helps to balance them when swimming. In cuttlefish, an adapted fin surrounds the body as a thin fringe.

Squid have perfected the art of jet-propelled swimming, thrusting themselves along by squirting water through a siphon at high speed. They are able to swivel the siphon to change direction and escape from attack. At slower speeds, squid and cuttlefish are propelled by a wave-like movement of their fin or fringe.

Cuttlefish are masters of the art of camouflage. They are able to change colour quickly to match their background, because thousands of their skin cells contain pigment, or colour. These cells are controlled by the cuttlefish's nervous system and can change the animal's colour in seconds.

▼ **Squid are longer and** thinner than cuttlefish, and many species have a triangular fin.

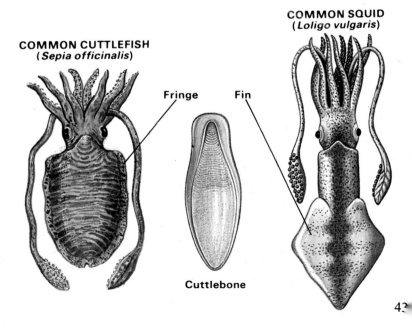

COMMON CUTTLEFISH
(*Sepia officinalis*)

COMMON SQUID
(*Loligo vulgaris*)

Fringe

Fin

Cuttlebone

Arthropods

With nearly 1 million species identified and named, and very probably several times that number still to be discovered, the phylum Arthropoda is the largest of all the animal phyla. There are 10 times as many arthropods as molluscs (the next largest phylum), for example, and over 20 times as many of them as there are vertebrates. Arthropods include insects, spiders and other arachnids, and crustaceans such as crabs and lobsters.

Arthropod features

The word arthro-pod means 'joint-limbed', and this is one of two features unique to the phylum. The other is a hard external covering known as an exoskeleton, which acts as a framework supporting the limbs in much the same way that the internal skeleton of a vertebrate does. Having this framework has allowed arthropods to develop limbs that can move rapidly, as well as to evolve a host of other special features, including wings for flight.

In some arthropod species the exoskeleton is hard enough to act as a suit of armour, protecting the soft body inside it from attack. Lobsters and crabs, and some beetles, have this type of tough exoskeleton, which thickens into a hard shield (called a carapace) on the body.

Their exoskeletons also prevent arthropods' bodies from drying out – which would happen if they were exposed to heat and air – and they are one reason why there are so many land-dwelling species within the phylum.

Living inside armour plating does have a major drawback though – it does not allow for growth. Arthropods have to break out of their exoskeletons from time to time so that they can grow bigger. This shedding process is known as moulting. When it happens, the arthropod absorbs some of its hard exoskeleton back into its body, then splits the remaining layers open. After this the animal wriggles free and grows a fresh exoskeleton, using internal air or fluid pressure to inflate its soft new covering to a larger size before it hardens.

◀ **An African species of** grasshopper moulting its old skin. Like all arthropod species, it has jointed limbs and a hard exoskeleton. Grasshoppers are jumpers, with strong hind limbs.

Phylum Arthropoda

- Jointed limbs
- Hard exoskeleton
- Known in all habitats

Table 2 – Arthropod groups

There are nearly 1 million arthropod species, grouped in nine classes. About 7000 new insect species are classified each year.

Rank	Common name	Species known
CLASS INSECTA	**Insects**	**c. 860,000**
Order Diplura	Diplurans	660
Order Collembola	Springtails	2000
Order Protura	Proturans	170
Order Thysanura	Silverfish, firebrats	350
Order Microcoryphia	Bristletails	420
Order Ephemeroptera	Mayflies	2000
Order Odonata	Dragonflies, damselflies	5000
Order Blattaria	Cockroaches	3500
Order Mantodea	Mantises	1800
Order Isoptera	Termites	2230
Order Zoraptera	Zorapterans	22
Order Grylloblattaria	Grylloblattids	12
Order Dermaptera	Earwigs	1200
Order Orthoptera	Grasshoppers & relatives	20,000
Order Phasmida	Stick & leaf insects	2500
Order Embioptera	Web spinners	170
Order Plecoptera	Stoneflies	3000
Order Psocoptera	Book lice	1700
Order Mallophaga	Biting lice	2600
Order Anoplura	Sucking lice	500
Order Thysanoptera	Thrips	5000
Order Hemiptera	Bugs	67,500
Order Coleoptera	Beetles, weevils	350,000
Order Strepsiptera	Stylopids	300
Order Hymenoptera	Bees, wasps, ants	120,000
Order Raphidioptera	Snake flies	80
Order Neuroptera	Lacewings & relatives	4500
Order Megaloptera	Alder flies	500
Order Mecoptera	Scorpion flies	400
Order Diptera	True flies	90,000
Order Siphonaptera	Fleas	1800
Order Trichoptera	Caddis flies	5000
Order Lepidoptera	Butterflies, moths	165,000
CLASS MEROSTOMATA	**Horseshoe/King crabs**	**5**

CLASS ARACHNIDA	Arachnids	c. 74,000
Order Scorpiones	Scorpions	1200
Order Uropygi	Whip scorpions	85
Order Schizomida	Schizomids	80
Order Amblypygi	Tail-less whip scorpions	70
Order Palpigradi	Micro-whip scorpions	60
Order Araneae	Spiders	35,000
Order Ricinulei	Ricinuleids	35
Order Pseudoscorpiones	False scorpions	2000
Order Solpugida	Wind/Sun scorpions	900
Order Opiliones	Harvestmen	4500
Order Notostigmata	Leathery mites	
Order Parasitiformes	Mites	} 30,000
Order Acariformes	Mites, ticks	
CLASS PYCNOGONA	**Sea spiders**	**1000**
CLASS CHILOPODA	**Centipedes**	**3000**
CLASS DIPLOPODA	**Millipedes**	**10,000**
CLASS SYMPHYLA	**Symphylans**	**160**
CLASS PAUROPODA	**Pauropods**	**500**
CLASS CRUSTACEA*	**Crustaceans**	**c. 39,150**
Subclass Cephalocarida	Cephalocarids	10
Subclass Branchiopoda	Water-fleas & relatives	850
Subclass Remipedia	Remipedians	9
Subclass Tantulocarida	Tantulocarids	10
Subclass Mystacocarida	Mystacocarids	10
Subclass Branchiura	Fish lice	150
Subclass Copepoda	Copepods	8400
Subclass Cirripedia	Barnacles & relatives	1000
Subclass Ostracoda	Mussel shrimps	5700
Subclass Malacostraca	Crabs, shrimps & relatives	23,000

*Because the class Crustacea contains such a variety of animals, the orders within it are grouped into ten subclasses.

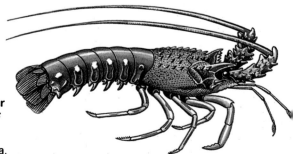

► **This Spiny lobster** or Crawfish (*Palinurus vulgaris*) is one of the crustacean species in the phylum Arthropoda.

Insects

Most arthropods – around 85 per cent, in fact – are grouped in the class Insecta. Insects range in size from tiny creatures like proturans and thrips, which are less than 1 mm long, to the huge tropical Goliath beetle (*Goliathus druryi*), which can grow to 20 cm and weigh as much as 100 grams!

All insects, no matter how big or small, have six legs arranged in three pairs. Their bodies are divided into three parts – a head, a thorax or chest, and an abdomen or stomach – and they usually have two pairs of wings. Apart from that, insects' body shapes vary tremendously, usually showing an adaptation to a particular habitat.

Most insects can fly, and they are the only invertebrate animals that do this. Flight allows insects to escape from enemies and to travel about in search of food. Some insects fly great distances and even migrate from one continent to another.

Changes of life

Many insect species have complex lifecycles and grow a completely new kind of body at different stages in their development from egg to adult. This process of change is called metamorphosis and there are two kinds – partial and complete.

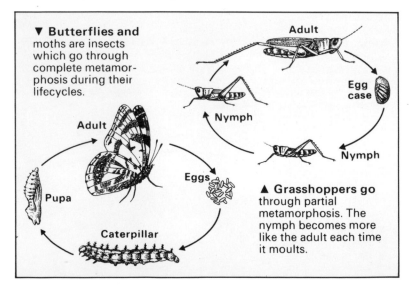

▼ **Butterflies and** moths are insects which go through complete metamorphosis during their lifecycles.

Adult

Egg case

Nymph

Nymph

▲ **Grasshoppers go** through partial metamorphosis. The nymph becomes more like the adult each time it moults.

Adult

Eggs

Pupa

Caterpillar

▶ **Leaf insects show** some of the finest body camouflage in the animal kingdom – their shape and colour helps them to hide from their enemies by blending into their surroundings. This leaf insect, *Bioculatum cifolium* from Java, has a flattened body and rims to its legs which look like leaves. It even has brown markings that resemble the damaged areas on a leaf.

In partial metamorphosis, the egg hatches into a wingless form called a nymph, which looks rather like a simplified version of the adult insect. The nymph grows and moults until it finally changes into the adult form. Orders that grow in this way include Odonata (dragonflies), Orthoptera (grasshoppers and relatives) and Hemiptera (bugs).

In complete metamorphosis, the egg hatches into a worm-like larva (plural larvae). This feeds and grows and then enters a resting stage; when it is called a pupa (plural pupae). The pupa doesn't eat, and after some time the adult emerges from it. Orders Coleoptera (beetles), Hymenoptera (bees and relatives), Diptera (true flies) and Lepidoptera (butterflies and moths) have complete metamorphosis.

The larvae of butterflies and moths are known as caterpillars, while the larvae of many other insect species are called grubs.

Class Insecta

- Body divided in three parts; abdomen doesn't bear legs
- Three pairs of legs
- Usually two pairs of wings, but some have one pair or none
- Mostly terrestrial; a few aquatic

Dragonflies

As members of the order Odonata, dragonflies are among the insects that undergo partial metamorphosis and have a different way of life in young and adult stages. Adult dragonflies spend most of their lives on the wing, but their nymphs live underwater not in the air. Depending on the particular species, the nymphs stay in the water for up to six years and go through several moults.

Adult dragonflies fly very fast (up to 54 km/h) and catch the insects on which they feed by chasing them on the wing. They are masters of the air and even stake out and defend breeding territories, much as birds do.

Butterflies and moths

These beautiful insects (order Lepidoptera) go through complete metamorphosis, from egg through larval and pupal stages. As adults, they feed on the nectar of flowers, sucking this food in through their long grooved mouthparts or proboscises (singular proboscis).

When fully opened, the wings of some butterflies and moths are very broad. The wingspans of the largest species, such as the beautiful Atlas moth (*Attacus*

▼ **Unlike those of butterflies** and moths, a dragonfly's wings are always spread in an open position. Even when a dragonfly is resting, its delicate wings cannot be folded against its body.

atlas) and birdwing butterflies (family Papilionidae) of South-East Asia, can be 25 cm.

There is enormous variety in the wing patterns of butterflies and moths. Some are drab and dull, but this makes the insect blend in with its background and prevents the birds that prey on it from spotting an easy meal. Other wing patterns are very vivid and showy, often with spots that look like eyes on the wings. Flashing these eyespots startles birds and other predators and often gives the insect time to escape. Some brightly coloured species, such as the Monarch butterfly (*Danaus plexippus*) of North America, are poisonous to other animals. The colours act as a warning and predators soon learn to steer clear.

The colour on moths' and butterflies' wings comes from the thousands of tiny scales which cover their surfaces. The wings of some species have a metallic sheen and colours that change with the angle of the light reflecting off them. This shininess is not caused by the colour of the scales themselves, but by the fine structure of their surfaces. A similar effect is created when light is reflected by oil floating on water.

▶ **The beautiful colours of** butterflies' and moths' wings come from tiny scales covering their surface. When fully opened, the wings of many species are very broad (average wingspan given in brackets).

Morpho butterfly
(*Morpho cypris*, 20 cm)

Monarch butterfly
(*Danaus plexippus*, 10 cm)

Small tortoiseshell butterfly
(*Aglais urticae*, 5 cm)

Spanish moon moth
(*Graellsia isabellae*, 8.5 cm)

51

Bugs

One of the main identifying features of these insects is their sharp, needle-like mouthparts, which they are expert at using to suck the juices from other animals or from plants. Bugs are grouped in the order Hemiptera and range in size from tiny aphids, 2–3 mm long, to giant waterbugs of the family Belostomatidae, some of which can grow to 11 cm.

The best-known bugs are probably the aphids (family Aphididae) – you may have seen huge numbers of them on garden plants such as roses and beans. An aphid feeds by piercing a plant's stem and sucking out the juice inside. Thousands of them all feeding together can seriously damage plants and even kill them, so aphids are considered serious pests by gardeners and farmers alike.

Aphids are capable of massive population explosions. These happen because the females give birth to baby aphids that are already carrying young of their own. The babies can give birth just ten days after they themselves are born.

Another member of the order Hemiptera is the pond-skater (family Gerridae), which has long slender legs and can walk on

◀ **Cicadas are large** bugs which feed by piercing the bark of trees with their sharp, needle-like mouthparts and sucking out sap. The mouthpart of this Dog-day cicada (*Tibicen caniculatus*) can be seen between its front limbs.

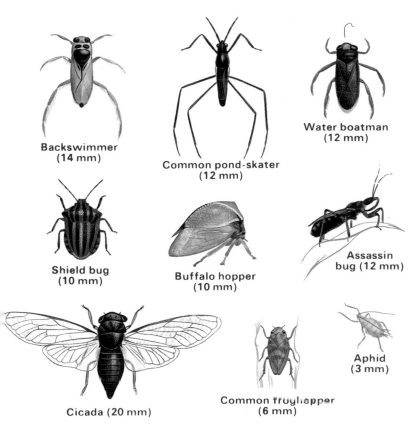

Backswimmer
(14 mm)

Common pond-skater
(12 mm)

Water boatman
(12 mm)

Shield bug
(10 mm)

Buffalo hopper
(10 mm)

Assassin
bug (12 mm)

Cicada (20 mm)

Common froghopper
(6 mm)

Aphid
(3 mm)

the surface of water. As their group name suggests, the back-swimmers (family Notonectidae) spend most of their lives upside down in ponds, while the adult froghoppers (family Cercopidae) are excellent jumpers. The nymphs of froghoppers live on plants in the frothy substance called cuckoo-spit.

The cicadas (family Cicadidae) are large bugs of the world's warmer regions, where the male's shrill song is a familiar summer sound. The most surprising thing about the cicada's

▲ **Many bugs, including** aphids, froghoppers and cicadas, feed by sucking juices from plants. Water boatmen and backswimmers are aquatic and feed mainly on invertebrates.

song is that it doesn't come from its mouth, but from vibrating drum-like areas on its body.

This fascinating insect is more often heard than seen, in fact. Cicadas spend their nymph stage underground, living there for several years, feeding on roots. They climb up into trees before emerging as adults.

53

▲ **The Rhinoceros beetle** (*Oryctes nasicornis*) is named because of the horn-like growth on its head.

◄ **A Seven-spot ladybird** (*Coccinella septempunctata*) about to land on flower heads. Beetles' hard forewings, or elytra, are held open during flight.

Beetles

Beetles are often confused with bugs, but their mouthparts are adapted for biting and are completely different from the needle-like mouthparts of bugs.

The name of the beetle order, Coleoptera, comes from *koleos*, which means 'shield' in Greek. Beetles have hard forewings called elytra (singular elytron) which act as shields for their folded delicate hindwings when they are not flying.

Although most beetle species can fly quite well, they spend much of their lives on or in the ground. You'll find them scrambling about in the roots of plants, or under stones and logs – places where their elytra help to protect them and stop their bodies from drying out. Diving beetles, such as members of the family Dytiscidae, hunt underwater for food and carry their own supply of air down with them under their wings.

Ladybirds (family Coccinellidae) are bright red, orange or yellow beetles with distinctive spots on their elytra. They are a common sight in gardens, where they and their larvae feed on other insect species, particularly aphids. The blood of ladybirds has a very nasty smell and taste, and their enemies learn to avoid the bright colours of these little beetles and to go for tastier prey. If attacked, a ladybird will squirt out some of its own blood in self-defence!

Friend and foe
Some beetles are serious pests. The black-and-yellow striped Colorado beetle (*Leptinotarsa decemlineata*), for example, can destroy potato crops. The Death-watch beetle (*Xestobium rufovillosum*) damages houses and furniture, as does the wood-worm, which is the larva of the Furniture beetle (*Anobium punctatum*).

Dung beetles (family Scarabaeidae) are altogether more useful. They have broad front legs with which they dig into the soil to bury dung, beginning a process that helps to recycle this waste material. The beetles lay their eggs in the dung, and their larvae feed on it after hatching.

Strange flashing lights on a summer's night may betray glow-worms (family Lampyridae) – a type of beetle, despite their name. Male glow-worms can fly, but the females are wingless and use their greenish lights to attract the males in the breeding season. The fireflies or lightning bugs belong to the same family. They behave in a similar way, except that both sexes can fly. These common names show one reason why scientific names are so necessary – these animals are neither worms, flies nor bugs!

▼ **Dung beetles are named** because they feed on dung and lay their eggs in it. The bright colours of these South African beetles (*Gymnopleurus virens*) are typical of many species.

True flies

The common Housefly (*Musca domestica*) is the most familiar member of this order, Diptera, which also includes horseflies, craneflies, mosquitos, hoverflies and fruitflies.

The word diptera means 'two wings', and whereas most other insects have four wings (in two pairs), true flies have only one pair. Their second pair has been reduced to modified wings called halteres. However, these club-shaped 'hindwings' appear to contribute to manoeuvrability in the air, as without their halteres flies lose their sense of balance and are unable to fly properly.

True flies can beat their wings very rapidly, and the buzzing or humming sounds they make are the result of these wing beats. Blowflies (family Calliphoridae) have been timed at 120 beats per second, and mosquitos (family Culicidae) can achieve a staggering 600 beats! As well as flying at speed, many true flies can hover with ease.

The delicate mosquito is a sort of flying drilling rig. It has sharp, needle-like mouthparts (rather like those of bugs), which it uses to drill a tiny hole in the skin of mammals and suck their blood.

◄ **The enormous** eyes of this horsefly almost meet at the top of its head. The eyes of true flies are actually made up of thousands of tiny individual lenses, each one contributing part of the whole view to the insect's brain.

▲ **The tiny modified** hindwings of true flies are called halteres. They help with balance in flight.

▶ **A female mosquito** sucks a meal of blood through its needle-like mouthparts.

Only the female mosquito actually sucks blood, and she needs this meal before laying her eggs. These are deposited like rafts, to float on the surface of still pools and ponds until they hatch into wriggling larvae.

Hoverflies (family Syrphidae) are well named, as they spend much of the time poised motionless in the air, their wings vibrat-ing rapidly to keep their bodies airborne but not taking them in any direction. Hoverflies look rather like bees or wasps, but they cannot sting and are quite harmless. Many types of hover-fly actually mimic particular bee or wasp species. Birds mistake these hoverflies for a real (and dangerous) bee or wasp and avoid making a meal of them.

57

Bees, wasps and ants

These insects belong to the order Hymenoptera. The word means 'membrane wing', and bees and wasps have two pairs of thin, transparent wings. Although most ants are wingless, they usually have a winged stage in their lifecycle. The bodies of most bees, wasps and ants are divided by a narrow 'waist' between the thorax and abdomen.

Bees and wasps, and some ant species, can sting when disturbed and this makes them dangerous in large numbers. The venom is actually injected via a modified egg-laying tube, and only the females can sting.

Some members of this order have developed complicated societies, in which hundreds, and sometimes thousands, of individuals live together, working for the good of the whole group. All ants, but only a few species of bee and wasp, are social insects.

Ants (family Formicidae) have one of the most cooperative lifestyles in the animal kingdom. Worker ants are always scampering about in platoons, gathering food, constructing nests, or defending them against intruders. For some time biologists were mystified about the way these insects communicate with each other to coordinate their behaviour. It is now known that ants rely largely upon chemical messages. Each ant produces a special substance, which the other ants can detect and follow. This is particularly helpful when ants are out hunting for food.

Army or driver ants (such as genera *Eciton*, *Anomma* and *Dorylus*) live in extremely large

▲ **Venezuelan Leaf-cutting** ants (genus *Atta*) on a leaf-collecting expedition.

◀ **Honeybees (*Apis mellifera*)** are social insects. Female bees do all the work around the hive, but only the queen lays eggs.

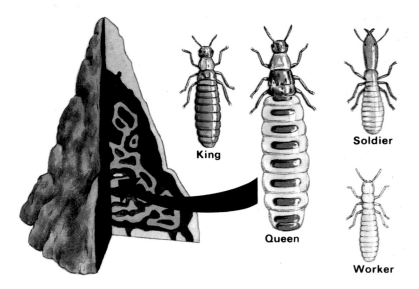

King

Queen

Soldier

Worker

▲ **Some termite mounds are** as high as 6 metres. A colony may contain over 1 million insects.

colonies, sometimes as many as 20 million strong. They hunt by sending out raiding parties, which attack and kill any suitable invertebrates (or even small vertebrates) that they come across. When the hunting is over they return to base, streaming along the chemical trails left on the way out.

Termites

Termites are grouped in the order Isoptera. Although they are not related to ants, termites have a similar – and in many ways even more extreme – social organization. A termite colony may contain more than 1 million individuals, with a king and a queen ruling over them.

Most termites in the colony look rather like ants and at 6 mm or so long are fairly small. The queen, however, is three or four times as large and has an expanded abdomen. Her enormous body is designed to keep on laying large numbers of eggs – her main activity for most of her life, which in some species can be 15 years long. Most of the other insects in the colony are the workers, which gather food and help with building, cleaning and repairing. The colony is guarded by fierce soldier termites, which have large biting jaws and can squirt poison at their enemies.

Several termite species make large mounds to house their colonies, and these can tower more than 6 metres above the ground. Termite mounds like this are a common feature in areas of Africa and Australia.

Spiders and relatives

With around 74,000 species, the arachnids are the second largest arthropod grouping after insects. Nearly half the arachnid species are spiders, but the class contains scorpions, ticks, and mites as well. Unlike insects, with their three-part bodies and three pairs of legs, most arachnids' bodies have two parts – a head and an abdomen – with four pairs of legs.

Arachnids are biters and have fanged jaws. Their fangs help them to catch their prey, and many species can also use them to inject a poisonous venom, which stuns and sometimes kills. Only a few spiders and scorpions are dangerous to humans, though.

Spiders (order Araneae) can be found in many different habitats – houses and gardens, woodland and grassland, there are even some that can dive under water. They are active creatures which feed mostly on insects, catching their meal either by chasing it or by trapping it in a web.

A spider constructs its web from silk, which it makes inside its body in special organs called spinnerets. It actually produces two different sorts of silk. One is a tough silk for the frame of the web, and the other is a stretchy, sticky silk which is woven into a spiral shape around the middle of the frame. When a fly blunders into a web, it gets stuck long

▶ A female Garden spider (*Araneus diadematus*) sits in her web, waiting for prey.

SPIDER RECORDS

Largest – the bodies of some bird-eating spiders grow to 9 cm. The legspan of the biggest species, *Theraphosa leblondi* of South America, can be 26 cm.

Most dangerous – the Black widow (*Latrodectus mactans*) can be fatal, but Australia's Funnel-web spider (*Atrax robustus*) is one of the most poisonous species.

Class Arachnida

- Body usually divided in two parts
- Four pairs of legs
- Jaws with fangs
- Mostly terrestrial

▲ **Scorpions have large claws** and a poisonous sting at the end of their tails. This small European species (*Euscorpius flavicaudus*) very rarely uses its sting, however. Like most scorpions it is active at night and catches and kills its insect prey in its claws.

enough for the spider to run out and bite it. The spider's venom paralyzes the fly while the spider wraps it in a silk bundle so that it cannot escape. When a web gets tattered the spider simply eats it and spins a new one!

Not all spiders spin webs. Trapdoor spiders such as members of the family Ctenizidae live in a burrow, for example, and cover the entrance with a hinged door made from soil and silk. The spiders sit inside their burrows, waiting until an insect walks past. Then they open the door and jump on the insect, dragging it back into the tunnel to kill and eat it.

Scorpions (order Scorpiones) look rather like long spiders, but their big lobster-like claws and arching tail make them even more ferocious. At the end of the tail is a poisonous sting which is used if the scorpion has to fight with its prey. Scorpions are typically found in hot dry countries, where they come out from under logs and stones in the cool of the night to hunt.

Centipedes and millipedes

Even though the word centipede means '100 legs', most species have between 15 and 23 pairs. The name millipede means '1000 legs' and is another exaggeration, since most species have fewer than 100 pairs. There are exceptions, though, and some centipedes (particular species grouped in the order Geophilomorpha, for example) have more than 170 pairs of legs, while some millipedes in the family Julidae have about 240 pairs.

The major difference between the two arthropod groups is that centipedes (class Chilopoda) have one pair of legs on each segment, whereas millipedes (class Diplopoda) have two. Centipedes have long legs and can run quickly to catch their prey or escape from enemies.

Class Chilopoda
- Segmented body, long and flattened
- Many legs; one pair per segment (to maximum of about 175 pairs)
- Fast running
- Long feelers on head
- Jaws with poison fangs
- Terrestrial

► ▼ **Centipedes'** front legs are used as jaws, while the last pair are often long and sensitive to touch, like the feelers on the head.

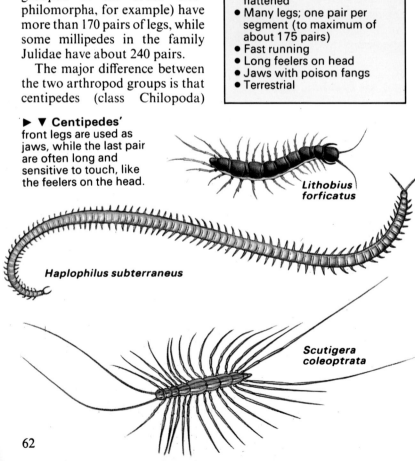

Lithobius forficatus

Haplophilus subterraneus

Scutigera coleoptrata

Defence and attack

Millipedes do not have long legs or speed to help them escape predators. Instead, they rely upon rolling their bodies up to protect themselves. The pill millipedes (family Glomeridae) are even able to roll themselves into a complete ball when disturbed.

Some millipedes can sweat a poison from their skin, and this also puts off their attackers. Tropical species within the family Julidae do more than sweat – they will spray their attackers with poison. Apart from this defence mechanism, millipedes are fairly harmless plant-eaters.

Centipedes, by contrast, feed on other small invertebrates, such as insects or slugs. Their first two legs are modified as poison fangs, and centipedes can use them to inject their prey with venom. After poisoning its victim, a centipede tears it apart with its jaws and sucks out its body fluids.

Most centipedes are too small to have a dangerous effect on humans, but tropical species such as *Scolopendra gigantea* of Central and South America grow to 30 cm long and include lizards, mice and even birds in their diet. These centipedes can give very painful bites if handled, and there are reports of people having been killed by them.

Class Diplopoda
- Segmented body, long and rounded
- Many legs; two pairs per segment (around 240 pairs maximum)
- Slow running
- Short feelers on head
- Terrestrial

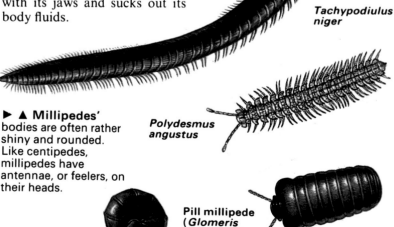

Tachypodiulus niger

Polydesmus angustus

▶ ▲ **Millipedes'** bodies are often rather shiny and rounded. Like centipedes, millipedes have antennae, or feelers, on their heads.

Pill millipede (*Glomeris marginata*)

Crustaceans

Just as insects have colonized every possible habitat on the land, crustaceans dominate the rivers and seas. From tiny transparent water-fleas, to shrimps, crabs and lobsters, they come in all shapes and sizes and are as common in salt water as they are in fresh.

Unlike insects and arachnids, crustaceans cannot be identified by a fixed number of legs. Instead they have several pairs of legs, which in different species have been adapted for swimming and even feeding. Their bodies are divided into head, thorax and abdomen and covered by a hard, crust-like carapace – their class name comes from the Latin word *crusta*, which means a rind or crust. The carapace is part of the exoskeleton and it is best developed in the crabs and lobsters. The exoskeleton of crustaceans is jointed to allow movement in the legs and abdomen.

Crustaceans have two pairs of feelers, or antennae (singular antenna), which grow forwards from the head. Usually, however, only one pair of antennae is visible.

Landlubbers

Woodlice (subclass Malacostraca) are among the few crustaceans that have managed to escape from the water and adapt to life on land. Even woodlice can only survive in moist conditions, though, and they die quickly if they get too dry.

The Robber crab (*Birgus latro*) is another crustacean that lives on dry land. It only returns to the sea to breed.

▲ The woodlouse *Porcellio scaber* is common in Europe. Woodlice grow to about 10 mm and have seven pairs of legs.

▶ **Lobsters are well protected** by their thick exoskeletons. Like crabs, they have four pairs of walking legs, with large pincers on the first pair.

Class Crustacea

- Body divided into head, thorax and abdomen
- Hard, jointed 'armour' on body, sometimes shell-like
- Several pairs of legs
- Two pairs of feelers
- Nearly all aquatic; a few terrestrial

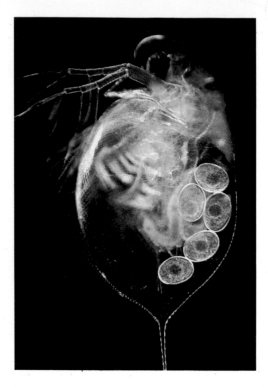

◄ **Water-fleas swim** by 'rowing' with their long antennae. Despite their name, they are crustaceans not insects. This female is carrying eggs – they can be seen through her transparent exoskeleton.

► **Barnacles open** their shells, and push out feathery legs to feed, only when submerged in water. They close up when the receding tide exposes them to air again.

Water-fleas and relatives

These tiny aquatic crustaceans are grouped in the subclass Branchiopoda, which means 'gillfoot' – their legs carry gills, through which they absorb oxygen from the water. The bodies of water-fleas are often transparent because their exoskeletons are very thin.

Water-fleas swim by beating their antennae, using their legs to absorb oxygen and to gather food particles from the water. The freshwater Fairy shrimp (*Chirocephalus diaphanus*) is the real expert when it comes to filter feeding. Large numbers of these creatures sometimes hatch out of eggs and appear in rainwater pools, where they are constantly on the move, swimming upside down and filtering food and oxygen from the water with their feathery legs.

A close relative of the Fairy shrimp, the Brine shrimp (*Artemia salina*), is one of the very few animals that can live in salt lakes, where the water is sometimes several times as salty as sea water. The eggs of Fairy and Brine shrimps can survive dry conditions for months, perhaps even years, and will still hatch out when put into water.

Barnacles

Barnacles and their relatives are grouped in the subclass Cirripedia. Many members of this subclass are parasites, which live in and feed on other animals, including crabs.

The barnacle itself is a most unlikely-looking crustacean. Indeed, it looks much more like a mollusc as it sits tightly attached to rocks at the seaside, protected by its shell. Its larvae give it away, however, as they look a bit like young water-fleas.

The adult barnacle cannot move, so it needs to be on rocks where waves constantly wash over it, bringing it food. Its larvae swim about in the sea searching for a suitable rock, usually settling on one where other barnacles are already attached. When it finds a good spot, the barnacle larva sticks its head to the rock by secreting a kind of glue. It then develops its shell. This is actually several hard chalky plates which surround the body, giving protection from predators and the waves. The adult barnacle uses its feet to filter the sea water for food, kicking them in and out of the gaps between the protective plates of its shell.

Barnacle colonies gather on rocks by the sea, but they also settle on wooden posts and even underneath boats. Be extra careful when clambering over rocks coated in barnacles, since the edges of this crustacean's hard plates are rather sharp.

▲ **Hermit crabs have** soft rear bodies, but don't grow a shell to protect themselves. Instead, they take over a mollusc's shell.

◄ **The Velvet** swimming crab (*Macropipus puber*) lives in rocky parts of the Atlantic coastline.

► **Krill (genus** *Euphausia*) are a kind of Antarctic shrimp. Like many other crustaceans, they use the feathery bristles on their legs to filter food from the water.

Crabs and lobsters

Many of the crustaceans in the subclass Malacostraca are good to eat, and for this reason they are sometimes called 'shellfish' – along with oysters, mussels, and other edible bivalves, which of course are molluscs! If you've ever eaten them, you'll know that both crabs and lobsters have extremely tough carapaces. This gives them protection from attack as they roam about the seabed in search of food.

Lobsters and crabs also have claws to protect themselves and catch food with. These are on their first pair of legs and the larger the species, the more fearsome-looking the claws. A lobster's diet includes soft molluscs, fish, and even crabs and other lobsters. Most crabs live in shallow water and often come out to look for food on the seashore. Some species are plant-eaters and feed on seaweeds, but many are active meat-eaters.

Crabs and lobsters have four pairs of walking legs, which crabs use to scuttle sideways, lobsters to crawl forwards.

Unlike lobsters and other crabs, hermit crabs (families Paguridae and Coenobitidae) cannot grow hard shells. Instead, they protect their soft bodies by living inside molluscs' shells – usually those of sea-snails. A hermit crab often takes over the empty shell of a dead animal, but it will also kill molluscs in order to invade their shells.

Shrimps and prawns

These crustaceans look like small delicate lobsters, but they are specialized for swimming rather than crawling along the seabed – they can actually do both, however. Shrimps and prawns feed on small invertebrates and seaweed, scavenging for them in the mud or sand. The smaller species are often found in rock pools.

Krill (genus *Euphausia*) are types of shrimp which occur in enormous swarms in the Southern Ocean. Although they are only 5 cm or so long, krill are the staple diet of some huge whale species. To satisfy their hunger, whales need to eat thousands of krill at a time – a medium-sized Blue whale eats 2 or 3 tonnes of krill in one meal! Krill are also the main food for a variety of seabirds, including penguins.

CRUSTACEAN RECORDS

Smallest – many of the water-fleas (order Cladocera) are less than 0.25 mm long, even as adults.

Largest – the Japanese spider crab (*Macrocheira kaempferi*) measures up to 3.7 metres across the span of its claws, although the smallest spider crab species are only 1 cm across.

Largest lobster – the North American species *Homarus americanus* can grow to 1 metre long and weigh 18 kg. It is also edible!

Starfish and Relatives

All members of this phylum, Echinodermata, live in the sea. They are very odd-looking creatures, largely because they do not have heads – in fact, in most species it is impossible even to tell the back from the front. This is because echinoderms have a wheel-like body plan, with five arms.

The phylum name comes from the words *echinos*, meaning 'hedgehog', and *derma* meaning 'skin'. It refers to the hard and sometimes spiny protective covering of these invertebrates. The spines project from an internal skeleton made of chalky plates, which is invisible in the living animal.

Their tube feet are unique to echinoderms. The tubes are extensions of a system of water channels which runs throughout their bodies. The tube feet can be extended by muscles that squeeze water into them. Suction is then used to grip the ground so that the body can be levered forwards. The tube feet are carefully coordinated to make the animal move slowly in one direction. A typical starfish (class Asteroidea) has about 1200 tube feet covering its underside.

A starfish will eat a variety of other animals, including fish, worms,

◄ **Starfish have five arms** which are covered with tiny tube feet on the underside.

▲ **A feather-star viewed from** above, showing its arms spread out in the water.

crustaceans, and even shelled molluscs. It eats a bivalve by attaching its tube feet to each shell and pulling to prise it open. The starfish then pushes its stomach inside the bivalve and digests it. One species, the Crown-of-thorns starfish (*Acanthaster planci*), feeds on corals and has destroyed large areas of Australia's Great Barrier Reef.

Feather-stars and brittle-stars

Most feather-stars (class Crinoidea) live rather like plants, attaching themselves to the seabed with a stalk which can be up to 1 metre long. There they collect in colonies, swaying about and filtering food from the water. Like starfish, feather-stars have arms, but in most species each arm is branched and rather feathery in appearance.

Brittle-stars have a small rounded body and long thin arms which wave in the water. They use their arms for walking and their tube feet just for feeding, unlike other echinoderms. As their common name suggests, brittle-stars' arms break off rather easily. Fortunately, they can replace them quickly by growing new ones. Brittle-stars are grouped in the class Ophiuroidea.

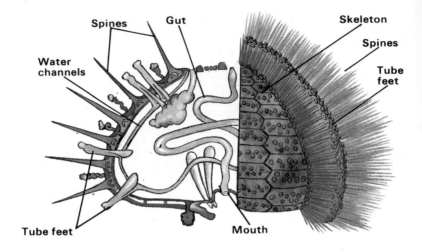

Spines Gut

Water channels

Skeleton

Spines

Tube feet

Tube feet

Mouth

Sea-urchins

The sharp spines of living sea-urchins make them look like animated pincushions. The chalky, ball-like skeletons of dead sea-urchins are more familiar to most people than the living creatures, however, as they are collected like shells and sometimes used as ornaments.

Dead sea-urchins look rather like starfish whose arms have been lifted and joined at the top to make a ball. If you look carefully at a sea-urchin's skeleton you will be able to see the phylum's typical five-rayed pattern quite clearly. Sea-urchins are grouped in the class Echinoidea.

Sand-dollars or sea-biscuits are kinds of sea-urchin which are found in shallow water off sandy shores. They live half-buried in the sand, filtering food particles from the water. They take their name from their flat shape – their skeletons look very like coins.

▲ **The hard chalky skeleton of** a living sea-urchin is covered in spines and tube feet.

Sea-cucumbers

These creatures are grouped in the class Holothuroidea and they are among the strangest of the echinoderms. They have the long bodies described by their name. Unlike typical echinoderms, they lack spines, although many species have small chalky ones embedded in their skin. They don't have a hard skeleton, and their skin is soft and leathery.

Like most other echinoderms, however, the majority of sea-cucumber species use their tube feet to move around. They spend their time creeping about on the seabed, using their tentacles to pick up food. In different species these tentacles are finger-like or feathery. They are moved by water pressure, in the same way as tube feet work.

▲ **An Australian species of** sea-urchin, *Echinothrix calamaris*. This species has particularly long and dramatically coloured spines.

▲ **The sea-cucumber** *Holothuria forskali* lives in the Atlantic Ocean. The feathery tube feet around its mouth are used for feeding.

▶ **Bêche-de-mer (*Stichopus variegatus*)** is a rare type of edible sea-cucumber.

Bridging the Gap

If you look back to Table 1, on page 17, you'll see that the phylum Chordata is divided into three subphyla. The largest of these is the Vertebrata, which contains all the animals with backbones. The other two subphyla, the Urochordata and the Cephalochordata, consist of animals that are invertebrates, but which show some features of the vertebrates. For this reason these two groups are seen as bridging the gap between animals without and with backbones.

Neither the Urochordata nor the Cephalochordata have a bony skeleton. However, they do share gill-like openings with the vertebrates, and running along the back, a nerve cord and a tube called a notochord.

The notochord is a sort of primitive backbone. It is a firm but flexible rod, to which muscles are attached, and it helps these invertebrates to swim. Many adult vertebrates have neither a notochord nor gill-slits, but these structures are always present in the growing stage before birth.

◄ **Adult sea-squirts (genus** *Ciona*). Water enters at the top. Food particles are strained from the water, which is then passed out through the spout on the side.

▲ **Two lancelets (genus** *Branchiostoma*) lie half buried in shell gravel, as they filter food from the water. Their heads are in the water, not the gravel.

The main group within the Urochordata is that of the sea-squirts (class Ascidiacea). The adult sea-squirt looks rather like a sponge, and like members of that phylum it filters its food from sea water. The sea-squirt's larva is quite different, however, and resembles a tiny tadpole, about 1 mm long. It is the larva that has the vertebrate features – the gill-slits, nerve cord and notochord.

There are only 25 species of Cephalochordata, and they are all lancelets. They look a bit like tiny fish larvae and they live their lives half buried in sand, filtering food from sea water. They can grow to about 10 cm and they occasionally swim rather jerkily to escape predators. Unlike fish, lancelets have no eyes, brain or fins.

Vertebrates

We tend to be much more familiar with vertebrates, the animals with backbones, than with invertebrates. This is partly because most vertebrates are large animals, but also because so many of them are land-dwelling species. The majority of the animals we keep as pets or see in farmyards and zoos are vertebrates.

There are five groups of vertebrates – fish, amphibians, reptiles, birds and mammals. Apart from fish, with their streamlined bodies and fins, most vertebrates have four limbs adapted for walking or swimming – even, in the case of birds and a few other animals, for gliding or flying.

All vertebrates have a strong internal skeleton which includes the backbone. The skeleton provides a rigid framework for the body and a firm anchor point for the muscles.

Another vertebrate feature is a nerve cord linked to a large brain, which is enclosed and protected by a skull of cartilage or bone. The brain works as a processing centre for information from sense organs like the eyes and ears, and this enables it to coordinate body movement. Their large brains allow vertebrates to think and react quickly to changes around them, and to have complex patterns of behaviour.

With around 21,500 species, fish are the largest vertebrate group, followed by birds with about 8800 and reptiles with around 6500. Amphibians and mammals have roughly the same number of species – 4000 or so each. Between them these five groups inhabit all corners of the planet, with fish the masters of the water and birds of the air.

▶ Leopards (*Panthera pardus*) are mammals, and like most species in this animal group they have a body covering of fur to keep them warm. The Leopard's spotted coat gives it good camouflage in dappled sunlight, as it waits to ambush its prey.

Fish

From the cold salt water of the Arctic and Antarctic to the warm fresh water of inland equatorial regions, the seas, rivers and lakes of our planet have been colonized by fish, the largest vertebrate group. They are divided into three classes – the jawless fish (class Agnatha), the cartilaginous fish (class Chondrichthyes), and the bony fish (class Osteichthyes).

Fish features
Fish have very muscular streamlined bodies and swim with a waving movement. They do this by contracting the muscles along each side of their body in turn – one side after the other. Their tail also helps to propel them forwards, by pushing against the water. The pairs of pectoral and pelvic fins act as balancers, although some fish also use these fins to help them move.

The skin of most fish species is covered with overlapping scales, which add to slipperiness in the water by giving a smooth body surface. The scales give protection because they are hard, but slide past each other so that the fish can bend easily as it swims.

Many bony fish have a special organ called the swim bladder. This lies near the gut and is like a tiny balloon filled with gases. Bony fish can alter the amount of gas in the swim bladder to enable them to float at any level in the water.

Fish have other special adaptations to underwater life. Some fish, such as lungfish (see page 85), have lung-like organs and can breathe air like humans and other land-dwelling vertebrates. However, most

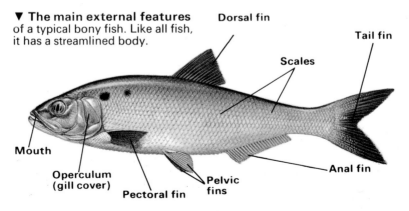

▼ **The main external features** of a typical bony fish. Like all fish, it has a streamlined body.

Dorsal fin

Tail fin

Scales

Mouth

Operculum (gill cover)

Pectoral fin

Pelvic fins

Anal fin

fish take oxygen from the water in which they live. Instead of lungs, they have feathery organs called gills which are lined with a network of thin-walled blood vessels. To breathe, a fish takes water into its mouth and passes it over its gills, where oxygen is transferred from the water into the blood. The water then leaves the fish's body through holes or slits at the side of its head.

Fish are cold-blooded animals, as are all invertebrates, amphibians and reptiles. Unlike the warm-blooded animals – birds and mammals – cold-blooded animals cannot easily control the temperature of their bodies or keep themselves warmer than their surroundings. An animal's body has to be at a certain temperature for its muscles and organs to operate properly, and if it is very cold, a cold-blooded animal slows down and its movements become sluggish.

Jawless fish

As their name suggests, unlike other fish the animals in this class do not have jaws. Jawless fish also lack paired fins and scales, and they have several sets of gills, each with a separate gill opening.

There are two sorts of jawless fish – lampreys (family Petromyzontidae) and hagfish (family Myxinidae).

Hagfish are very slimy animals which live at the bottom of the sea, where they eat dead or dying fish. They cut a hole through the skin, slither inside the fish and eat the insides. Even though hagfish don't have jaws, they have sharp teeth which can be pushed in and out of their mouths as they feed. Their skin produces slime which helps them slip into their prey and also protects them from attack.

Lampreys are parasites which feed by attaching themselves to a living fish and sucking its blood. They use special sharp teeth to rasp at their prey's skin until it bleeds.

▶ **Lampreys have seven gill** openings. This is the Brook lamprey (*Lampetra planeri*).

Class Agnatha
- Simple skeleton of cartilage
- No scales
- Jawless
- Eel-like shape
- Many pairs of gills for breathing
- Cold-blooded
- Aquatic

Table 3 – Fish groups

Fish classification is extremely complicated. New relationships are still being discovered and biologists are not yet agreed on a system.

Rank	Common name	Species known
CLASS AGNATHA	**Jawless fish**	**72**
Family Petromyzonidae	Lampreys	40
Family Myxinidae	Hagfish	32
CLASS CHONDRICHTHYES	**Cartilaginous fish**	**711**
Order Selachii	Sharks & dogfish	370
Order Batoidea	Rays, skates	318
Order Chimaeriformes	Chimaeras/Rabbit fish	23
CLASS OSTEICHTHYES	**Bony fish**	**c. 20,730**
Subclass Dipnoi	Lungfish	6
Subclass Crossopterygii	Lobe-finned fish	1
Subclass Actinopterygii*	Ray-finned fish	c. 20,725
Order Polypteriformes	Bichirs	10
Order Acipenseriformes	Sturgeons, paddlefish	27
Order Semionotiformes	Garpikes	7
Order Amiiformes	Bowfin	1
Superorder Clupeomorpha (1)	Herrings, anchovies & relatives	342
Superorder Elopomorpha (3)	Eels, tarpons & relatives	632
Superorder Osteoglossomorpha (2)	Bony-tongues, elephant fish	116
Superorder Protacanthopterygii (4)	Salmon, pike & relatives	990
Superorder Ostariophysi (4)	Carps, catfish & relatives	6000
Superorder Paracanthopterygii (6)	Cods & relatives	1100
Superorder Atherinomorpha (3)	Flying fish & relatives	1000
Superorder Acanthopterygii (11, including)	Spiny-finned fish	10,500
Order Perciformes	Perch, mackerel & relatives	8000
Order Scorpaeniformes	Scorpionfish, stonefish	1000
Order Pleuronectiformes	Flatfish	500
Order Tetraodontiformes	Puffer fish, box fish	330
Order Gasterosteiformes	Sticklebacks & relatives	250
Order Beryciformes	Pine-cone fish & relatives	180

*Because there are so many orders in the ray-finned fish, some related orders are combined into larger groups called superorders. The number of orders is given in brackets after each superorder name.

► **A clownfish**
(*Amphiprion clarkii*)
sheltering in the
tentacles of a sea-
anemone. Unlike most
animals, clownfish are
not harmed by the
anemone's stings.
Clownfish are grouped
with other bony fish, in
the class Osteichthyes.

▼ **A Grey reef shark**
(*Carcharinus ambly-
rhynchus*) cruises over
a bed of corals. Sharks
are cartilaginous fish,
grouped in the class
Chondrichthyes.

Cartilaginous fish

The best-known members of this group are the sharks, but it also contains dogfish, which look like small sharks, and skates and rays, which are a bit like sharks that have been rolled flat. Sharks and dogfish belong to the order Selachii, while skates and rays are grouped in the order Batoidea.

The skeletons of all these fish are made of cartilage, not bone. Cartilage is not as strong as bone, but it still provides a stiff skeleton.

Many cartilaginous fish are meat-eaters and have rows of very sharp teeth for tearing off chunks of flesh. Indeed, there can

be up to 3000 teeth in a shark's mouth. They are continuously replaced as they are worn down, and a shark may have as many as 20,000 teeth during its life.

A shark's lower teeth are rather thin and spiky, but its upper ones are triangular and very sharp. When a shark bites, it tears the flesh of its prey either by shaking its head from side to side, or by rolling over. Both these methods make the shark's upper teeth slash a deep groove.

There are about 370 species of shark. Although most are quite harmless to people, several species occasionally attack swim-

Spiny dogfish (*Squalus acanthias*)

Whale shark (*Rhincodon typus*)

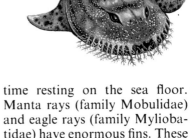

Wobbegong (*Orectolobus maculatus*)

▲ **Although the Whale shark** grows to 15 metres, it feeds by filtering small invertebrates from sea water. The other two fish are flesh-eaters.

◄ **A manta ray or devil fish** flaps gracefully through the sea. This shark relative can be 9 metres, measured across its fins.

mers. The most dangerous are the Great white shark (*Carcharodon carcharias*), the Mako shark (*Isurus oxyrinchus*) and the Tiger shark (*Galeocerdo cuvier*).

'Flying' fish

Cartilaginous fish have no swim bladder to help them float. In fact, if these fish stop swimming they sink to the seabed. A shark's body is lifted up as it swims by its fins, in much the same way as an aeroplane's wings help it stay in the air.

Rays and skates move by rippling their enlarged fins, but most species spend much of their time resting on the sea floor. Manta rays (family Mobulidae) and eagle rays (family Myliobatidae) have enormous fins. These fish can actually flap their wing-like fins up and down, so that they 'fly' through the water.

Class Chondrichthyes

- Skeleton of cartilage
- Rough skin, with toothed scales
- Paired fins
- Gill slits for breathing
- Meat-eating, with sharp teeth
- Cold-blooded
- Aquatic; mostly marine

Bony fish

All members of this class have a skeleton made of bone, like most other vertebrates, and this sets them apart from jawless fish and cartilaginous fish. Bony fish can also be distinguished from the other two fish classes by the flaps called opercula (singular operculum) which cover their gills.

Over 95 per cent of all fish species are bony fish. They range from tiny fish 2 cm long, to the sturgeons and catfish, which can grow to several metres. The class is so varied that it is further divided into three subclasses – lungfish (subclass Dipnoi), lobe-finned fish (subclass Crossopterygii) and ray-finned fish (subclass Actinopterygii).

Lobe-fins and lungfish

There is only one lobe-finned species in fact, and that is the Coelacanth (*Latimeria chalumnae*). It has a subclass all to itself because it is so different from all other living fish. We now know that the Coelacanth lives in deep water off the south-east coast of Africa, but before it was sighted in 1938 it was thought to have become extinct 65 million years ago, at about the same time as the dinosaurs disappeared.

The Coelacanth and the lungfish have fleshy fins, which are almost like very simple limbs. Although some lungfish can use these fins like legs to move along the mud at the bottom of ponds, they cannot support their weight outside the water.

Bony fish are found in all types of fresh and salt water – there are even species that can survive long periods outside the water altogether. Some lungfish species, for example, burrow into the mud if their pond begins to dry up. These lungfish can remain inside their mud cocoons for as long as four years!

Lungfish can survive out of water because they have lungs and gills. As well as absorbing oxygen from water through their gills, they can use their lungs to get oxygen from air. There are just six species and they all inhabit hot regions – the Amazon river of South America, and rivers in Africa and Australia.

▶ **The Queensland lungfish** (*Neoceratodus forsteri*) is only found in certain rivers and lakes in north-eastern Australia.

Class Osteichthyes
- Skeleton of bone
- Smooth skin, with bony scales
- Paired fins
- Gills covered by opercula
- Cold-blooded
- Aquatic (marine and freshwater)

▲ **Rainbow trout** (*Salmo gairdneri*) live in the sea and in freshwater lakes and rivers.

▼ **Plaice** (*Pleuronectes platessa*) live on the seabed.

◄ **Mackerel** (*Scomber scombrus*) inhabit coastal waters.

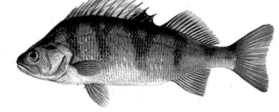

► **The Perch** (*Perca fluviatilis*) is a spiny-finned freshwater fish, which lives in lakes and rivers and feeds on smaller fish and invertebrates.

Ray-finned fish

Nearly all bony fish belong to the ray-finned subclass – there are around 20,725 species, in fact, grouped in 38 orders. As the table on page 80 shows, related orders are combined into larger groups called superorders, with around 50 per cent of species contained in the spiny-finned fish (Acanthopterygii).

As their name implies, the fins of these fish are thin sheets of skin, strengthened by bony rays. They are not fleshy like the fins of lungfish and lobe-fins, but delicate and fan-like, and they can be spread open or closed up.

The variety of ray-finned fish is quite staggering. They are found in the depths of the ocean, as well as in the surface layers of the sea and in rivers, ponds and lakes. In shape they range from the familiar Goldfish (*Carassias auratus*), to flattened species like Plaice (*Pleuronectes platessa*) and the Angelfish (*Pterophyllum scalare*) and the long wriggly eels (family Anguillidae).

Food from the ocean

Many ray-finned fish are good to eat. Some species are easy to catch because they swim about the sea in large groups called shoals or schools. Cod (*Gadus morhua*) and Herring (*Clupea harengus*) are among those caught in large numbers from fishing boats, and whole industries have grown up around them.

Flatfish like Plaice and Sole (*Solea solea*) are also fished commercially. They are not flat when they first hatch. As a young flatfish grows, its eyes move to one side of the head and its body flattens, with the side with the eyes getting darker to become the top. Adult flatfish are therefore really swimming on one side.

Two more tasty ray-fins are both members of the family Scombridae. Tuna are large muscular fish of the open ocean – some species reach 4 metres in length. Mackerel are very active fish which spend nearly all their time swimming. It is thought that mackerel never stop moving, in fact, and that by keeping their mouths open they allow water to flow over their gills automatically. Slower-moving fish breathe by gulping in mouthfuls of water. Like sharks, mackerel lack a swim bladder and only their speed stops them sinking.

▶ **The Cuckoo wrasse** (*Labrus mixtus*) feeds on crustaceans and molluscs and has strong teeth.

◀ **Seahorses** (genus *Hippocampus*) are related to sticklebacks. A seahorse swims slowly in an upright position, beating its dorsal fin so rapidly that it looks like a propeller. When still, it curls its tail around sea plants for support.

▼ **The Three-spined stickleback** (*Gasterosteus aculeatus*) has sharp spines on its back, which help to deter predators.

▲ **Eels (*Anguilla anguilla*)** spend part of their lives at sea and part in streams and rivers.

The hunters

There are some very unusual ray-fins. Angler fish (order Lophiiformes) attract their prey with a 'rod and line' which grows forward from the top of the head and even has a false bait. Smaller fish see this waving about and are snapped up when they approach to investigate. One species of angler fish has gone a stage further – its bait is actually inside its mouth. When its prey reaches the bait, this angler fish simply has to close its mouth to catch it.

Archer fish (family Toxotidae) live in rivers and swamps in South-East Asia, India and Australia. They have long tube-like mouthparts which they use rather like pea-shooters to knock insects into the water by firing water drops at them.

The Electric eel (*Electrophorus electricus*) and its relatives use specially adapted cells to generate an electric shock to deter enemies and attack prey. An Electric eel can produce up to 500 volts, which is enough to stun even a large mammal!

Fish out of water

Flying fish (family Exocoetidae) live near the surface of the sea. What makes them unusual is their 'wings' – a pair of large, expandable fins on the chest, which enable them to glide above the water surface. Flying fish cannot stay airborne long, however, and they do not flap their 'wings'. We don't know why they leap out of the water and glide, but it may be to escape from predators.

Both the mudskippers (genus *Periophthalmus*) and the Climbing perch (*Anabas testudineus*) spend much of their time out of the water. These fish balance on their front fins and get about by wriggling and jumping.

FISH RECORDS

Smallest – the Philippine goby (*Pandaka pygmaea*) reaches just 12 mm in length.

Largest – the Whale shark (*Rhincodon typus*) can be as much as 12 metres long.

Largest bony fish – a sturgeon, the Beluga (*Huso huso*) of the Caspian Sea, can grow to 8.5 metres in length.

Largest freshwater fish – the Arapaima (*Arapaima gigas*), which lives in the Amazon river of South America, grows to 4.5 metres.

Fastest – the marlin family includes the Sailfish (*Istiophorus platypterus*), which achieves speeds of about 80 km/h. Other speed champions are the Swordfish (*Xiphius gladius*), which is capable of 90 km/h, and the Mako or Blue pointer shark (*Isurus oxyrinchus*), which can swim at 96 km/h!

▲ **As well as feeding in the** usual way underwater, archer fish have a unique way of catching their prey. They fire water drops at insects to knock them off their perch and bring them within eating range!

▶ **Mudskippers can breathe** out of water as well as in it. They inhabit mangrove swamps in West Africa, South-East Asia and Australia, crawling over the mud on their fleshy pectoral fins. The mudskippers shown here (*Periophthalmus chrysospilos*, from Malaysia) have even climbed the stem of a mangrove tree.

Class Amphibia

- Skin not waterproof
- Jelly-like eggs
- Aquatic larvae (tadpoles)
- Breathe through skin, gills or lungs
- Cold-blooded
- Terrestrial and aquatic

▲ **This European frog (*Rana temporaria*)** has the soft moist skin typical of amphibians. Adult frogs can absorb oxygen through their skin, as well as breathing air into their lungs.

Amphibians

The word amphibian means something that is equally at home on land and in water, and this double lifestyle is a characteristic of most members of the class Amphibia.

Amphibians are cold-blooded, like fish, and in very cold weather their bodies slow down and they become sluggish. In countries with hard winters, some species become inactive during the cold and enter a kind of deep sleep called hibernation. They may hide under a log, or in leaf litter, or bury themselves in mud at the bottom of a pond. Often they stay asleep like this, without feeding, until the weather gets warmer again.

Most amphibians undergo a metamorphosis, as insects do, changing body shape completely between young and adult form. There are three orders – the caecilians (order Apoda), the salamanders and newts (order Urodela), and the frogs and toads (order Anura). Salamanders and newts have tails and can swim like fish by wriggling their bodies from side to side. They use a similar movement to crawl on land, as their legs are rather weak. Frogs and toads have longer legs and swim by kicking backwards. On land they jump or crawl, although some species can climb.

Caecilians

These peculiar legless amphibians look rather like large earthworms. The various species range from 7 cm to 1.5 metres long.

Caecilians like warm climates and are found in tropical forests and streams, where they burrow about in soft mud and soil, looking for small animals such as worms and insects to eat. Sometimes they even eat small lizards, grabbing them in their powerful jaws.

Like most other amphibians, caecilians have smooth slimy skin which needs to be kept moist. This usually restricts them to wet or damp habitats.

▲ **At first sight caecilians** look like large earthworms. They are almost blind, have no legs, and spend their lives burrowing in damp soil. This colourful species, *Caecilia tentaculata*, lives in tropical forests in French Guiana.

Table 4 – Amphibian groups

There are around 4000 species of amphibian, grouped in three orders and 34 families.

Rank	Common name	Species known
ORDER APODA (5 families)	**Caecilians**	**163**
ORDER URODELA	**Salamanders, newts & relatives**	c. **350**
Family Cryptobranchidae	Giant salamanders	3
Family Hynobiidae	Asiatic salamanders	33
Family Salamandridae	Newts, brook-salamanders & fire-salamanders	53
Family Amphiumidae	Amphiumas	3
Family Proteidae	Olm, mudpuppy, waterdogs	6
Family Ambystomatidae	Mole-salamanders	35
Family Dicamptodontidae	Pacific mole-salamanders	3
Family Plethodontidae	Lungless salamanders	209
Family Sirenidae	Sirens	3
ORDER ANURA	**Frogs & toads**	c. **3500**
Family Leiopelmatidae	Tailed frogs	4
Family Discoglossidae	Fire-bellied toads, midwife toads & relatives	14
Family Pipidae	Clawed & Surinam toads	26
Family Rhinophrynidae	Burrowing toad	1
Family Pelobatidae	Spadefoot toads, horned toads & relatives	88
Family Bufonidae	Toads	339
Family Brachycephalidae	Gold frogs	2
Family Rhinodermatidae	Mouth-brooding frogs	2
Family Heleophrynidae	Ghost frogs	4
Family Myobatrachidae	Myobatrachid frogs	100
Family Leptodactylidae	Leptodactylid frogs	722
Family Dendrobatidae	Arrow-poison frogs	116
Family Hylidae	Tree frogs	637
Family Centrolenidae	Glass frogs	64
Family Pseudidae	Pseudid frogs	4
Family Ranidae	Frogs	611
Family Sooglossidae	Seychelles frogs	3
Family Hyperoliidae	Sedge & bush frogs	292
Family Rhacophoridae	Old World tree frogs	184
Family Microhylidae	Narrow-mouthed frogs	281

▲ **A brightly coloured arrow-**poison frog sits on the leaf of a rainforest tree. As their name suggests, these beautiful frogs can be highly poisonous. They are grouped in the order Anura, family Dendrobatidae.

Frogs and toads

Although there is really no clear difference between frogs and toads, the species that live in water and have smooth skin are usually called frogs. The fat, warty-skinned species that live in damp places are called toads.

Frogs and toads have three different ways of breathing. In the tadpole stage of their metamorphosis from young to adult form, they live in water and use their feathery gills as fish do. As adults, they either use their lungs or absorb oxygen from the air directly through their moist skin.

Tropical frogs

The croaking of frogs at a breeding pond is a familiar if not very musical sound. Some of the tropical frogs are less hard on the ear, however, and make a wide range of calls which are very like those of birds. The males of a number of species gather at ponds in the breeding season and fill the air with a deafening chorus of croaks, clicks and whistles.

Somehow the females manage to filter out the special call of their own species and move towards it.

Besides songs for attracting a mate, these tropical frogs also have warning songs and ones for marking out their territory.

Tree frogs (family Hylidae) are another mainly tropical group. They are agile climbers which spend most of their time balanced in twigs and tree branches. To help them climb they have sticky pads on their fingers. The loose skin on their bellies also helps to stick them to smooth surfaces.

Arrow-poison frogs (family Dendrobatidae) live in the rainforests of South and Central America. They are small and brightly coloured (see page 93) – there are even some golden species. The venom in their skin is one of the most poisonous substances known, and the frogs received their name because they are a source of poison for arrows used in hunting by Indian tribes.

Frogspawn

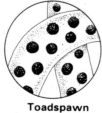

Toadspawn

There is a clear difference between the eggs, or spawn, of European frogs and toads. Toads lay their spawn in long thin strings, while frogs lay large clumps of individual eggs.

► An Eastern spade-foot toad (*Scaphiopus holbrookii*) of North America. These toads use their spade-like hind feet to dig burrows to live in.

▼ The African clawed toad (*Xenopus laevis*) rarely leaves the water, even when adult. It has big lungs and can survive in stagnant pools where the water has little oxygen. It can change its body colour to match that of its surroundings.

Newts and salamanders

These animals are rarely seen, mainly because they tend to spend their lives hidden away in places that are dark, cool and damp. They have small legs and cannot jump, and they move on land with short clumsy steps. Newts and salamanders have tails even as adults, unlike frogs and toads which lose their tails when their bodies change during metamorphosis.

Some species of salamander – such as the milky coloured Olm (*Proteus anguinus*) of Yugoslavia – are blind and live in the perpetual darkness of underground rivers and pools. These salamanders do not need to see, because vision is not possible in places where there is no light.

Newts are actually a type of salamander. Both animals look very similar, but unlike most salamanders, newts have flattened tails. Although this makes them particularly good swimmers, newts spend part of their adult lives on land, returning to water to breed in the spring.

The most attractive species of salamander are very brightly coloured – often red or yellow and black. It may seem odd that salamanders have these markings, as they make it easier for enemies to spot and attack them. The bright colours nearly always go with nasty poison glands in the salamanders' skin, however, and predators learn soon enough to leave them well alone.

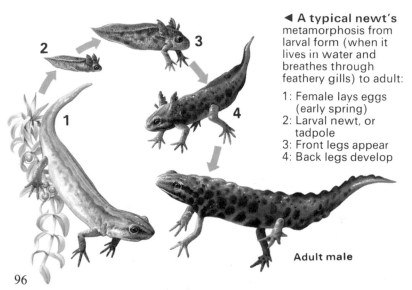

◄ **A typical newt's** metamorphosis from larval form (when it lives in water and breathes through feathery gills) to adult:

1: Female lays eggs (early spring)
2: Larval newt, or tadpole
3: Front legs appear
4: Back legs develop

Adult male

◄ **The bright colours** of the Fire salamander (*Salamandra salamandra*) are a warning of the unpleasant chemicals produced in its skin. Predators soon learn not to attack it.

► **A lungless** salamander crawls over wet moss – the species shown here is the Cave salamander (*Eurycea lucifuga*). As adults, lungless salamanders have neither gills nor lungs, and they breathe through their skin. To do this, their skin must be kept moist at all times and lungless salamanders are therefore only found in streams, or in very damp woodland.

Reptiles

Unlike fish and amphibians, few reptiles depend upon water for their survival. Their dry and scaly skin is waterproof, which stops moisture evaporating from their bodies. For this reason, reptiles do well in dry habitats like deserts where water is scarce.

Reptiles welcome the sun because they are cold-blooded and become slow-moving and inactive in cold weather. They speed up again in warm conditions, and lizards in particular spend a lot of time sunbathing to regulate their body temperature.

Although most reptiles lay eggs, quite a lot of lizard and snake species give birth to live young. Unlike amphibians, they lay their eggs on land – even turtles do this, although they spend the rest of their lives in the water. Reptiles' eggs are not hard and chalky like those of birds, but softer and rather leathery in texture. There is no larval stage and the young that hatch from the eggs look like miniature adults, as the photograph on page 101 shows.

The 6500 or so species of reptile are divided into four orders. These are tortoises and turtles (order Chelonia), lizards and snakes (order Squamata), crocodylians (order Crocodylia) and the dragon-like Tuatara (order Rhyncocephalia).

There is only one Tuatara species – *Sphenodon punctatus*. It is often described as a living fossil, because it is almost identical to reptiles that became extinct 140 million years ago.

Class Reptilia
- Dry scaly skin
- Most lay large leathery eggs
- No larval stage
- Breathe through lungs
- Cold-blooded
- Mostly terrestrial

▲ **Chameleons are a** type of lizard. Their tongues are attached to the front of their mouths and can be flicked forwards to catch their insect prey. This is the Mediterranean chameleon (*Chameleo chameleon*).

◄ **The Tuatara** (*Sphenodon punctatus*) is only found on certain islands off New Zealand's North Island. Tuataras grow very slowly and can live to be over 100 years old.

Table 5 – Reptile groups

Rank	Common name	Species known
ORDER CHELONIA	**Turtles & tortoises**	**244**
Family Chelidae	Side-necked turtles	37
Family Pelomedusidae	Side-necked turtles	24
Family Carettochelidae	Pig-nosed soft-shell turtle	1
Family Chelydridae	Snapping turtles	2
Family Dermatemydidae	C American river turtle	1
Family Cheloniidae	Sea turtles	6
Family Dermochelyidae	Leatherback sea turtle	1
Family Emydidae	Pond & river turtles	85
Family Kinosternidae	American mud & musk turtles	20
Family Staurotypidae	Mexican musk turtles	3
Family Testudinidae	Tortoises	41
Family Trionychidae	Soft-shell turtles	22
Family Platysternidae	Big-headed turtle	1
ORDER SQUAMATA	**Snakes, lizards, & worm-lizards**	**c. 6300**
Suborder Amphisbaenia (4 families)	Worm-lizards	140
Suborder Sauria	Lizards	3757
Family Agamidae	Chisel-teeth lizards	*300*
Family Chamaeleontidae	Chameleons	*85*
Family Iguanidae	Iguanas	*650*
Family Gekkonidae	Geckos	*800*
Family Pygopodidae	Snake lizards	*31*
Family Teiidae	Whiptails, racerunners	*227*
Family Lacertidae	Wall & sand lizards	*200*
Family Xantusiidae	Night lizards	*16*
Family Scincidae	Skinks	*1275*
Family Cordylidae	Girdle-tailed lizards	*50*
Family Dibamidae	Blind lizards	*4*
Family Xenosauridae	Xenosaurs	*4*
Family Anguidae	Anguids	*75*
Family Helodermatidae	Beaded lizards	*2*
Family Lanthanotidae	Bornean earless lizard	*1*
Family Varanidae	Monitor lizards	*37*
Suborder Serpentes	Snakes	2389
Family Pythonidae	Pythons	*27*
Family Aniliidae	Pipesnakes	*11*

Suborder Serpentes cont.		
Family Tropidophiidae	Protocolubroids	*22*
Family Boidae	Boas	*39*
Family Uropeltidae	Shieldtail snakes	*44*
Family Leptotyphlopidae	Thread snakes	*78*
Family Anomalepidae	Dawn blind snakes	*20*
Family Typhlopidae	Blind snakes	*163*
Family Colubridae	'Harmless' snakes	*1562*
Family Elapidae	Front-fanged snakes	*236*
Family Viperidae	Vipers	*187*
ORDER RHYNCOCEPHALIA (1 family)	**Tuatara**	**1**
ORDER CROCODYLIA	**Crocodylians**	**22**
Family Alligatoridae	Alligators & caimans	7
Family Crocodylidae	Crocodiles	14
Family Gavialidae	Gharial	1

▼ A Blue-tongued skink
(*Tiliqua nigrolutea*) with its
young. Skinks are a type of lizard
and they are classified in the
family Scincidae, order Squamata.

Tortoises and turtles

Most of the 40 or so land dwelling species in the order Chelonia are called tortoises. The remaining 200 or so species live in water and only return to land to breed. Aquatic species are called turtles, although some freshwater ones are known as terrapins.

Tortoises move slowly, as do turtles when on land. Although some species are very big – the Leatherback turtle (*Dermochelys coriacea*) can reach 2.7 metres and the Aldabra giant tortoise (*Geochelone gigantea*) 1.5 metres – their slowness makes them vulnerable to attack and they therefore usually have hard shells to protect them. When danger threatens, a turtle or tortoise simply pulls its legs and head inside its shell and waits until it is safe to come out again.

As their name suggests, soft-shell turtles (families Carettochelidae and Trionychidae) are exceptions to the rule. Their shells are too weak to give much protection, and these turtles spend most of their lives in the relative safety of the water. They have long necks and tube-shaped

▼ **Although turtles are** graceful and agile in water, they are slow and clumsy on land.

noses. This allows them to breathe while submerged – they just poke their nose above the water surface, like a snorkel.

Neither tortoises nor turtles have teeth. Instead, their mouths are horny and beak-like, and some species have an extremely hard bite. Tortoises mainly eat grasses, leaves, fruit and other plant food. However, turtles and terrapins are meat-eaters and will take a wide range of animals, including fish, molluscs and crustaceans such as crabs.

The snapping turtles (family Chelydridae) are fierce predators which live in the rivers of North and Central America. They have large jaws and can catch and eat fish, and even birds. One species, the Alligator snapping turtle (*Macroclemys temminckii*), lures fish right into its mouth with a false bait – a red worm-like growth on its tongue.

Starting out in life

Tortoises and turtles lay their eggs in sand or other soft soil. When the young hatch they dig their way up to the surface.

Sea turtles like the Loggerhead (*Caretta caretta*) come ashore to lay their eggs on sandy beaches. The female digs a nest hole into which she lays a large number of soft white eggs. She then fills in the hole and leaves the eggs to hatch by themselves. The baby turtles all hatch at the same time, hundreds making their way together as fast as possible to the safety of the sea. This is a dangerous time for the tiny turtles. Many do not make it and are picked off by hungry seabirds hovering overhead.

▼ **Turtles live in the sea but** come ashore to lay their eggs. This female Green turtle (*Chelonia mydas*) has dug a nest hole in the sand and is laying eggs into it.

Lizards

Lizards make up over half of all reptile species and range in size from tiny geckos only 15 mm long, to the large and fearsome monitor lizards (family Varanidae) which can sometimes grow to 3 metres.

Most lizard species prefer dry habitats and are active during the day. The geckos (family Gekkonidae) are an exception, since they are busiest during the night when their large eyes help them to see. Geckos have another unusual quality. They can climb straight up or down a vertical wall or window, or even across a ceiling. Special pads on their toes stick them firmly to even the smoothest surfaces.

Another lizard group, the chameleons (family Chamaeleontidae), have an unusual way of hunting. They clamber very slowly among twigs and other vegetation, altering their body

▶ **Supported by its** special toe pads, a Tokay gecko (*Gekko gecko*) clings upright to a plant.

▼ **Because of their** toe pads, geckos can run straight up a wall, or even upside down across a ceiling. The ridges on their toes branch into tiny bristles, each one ending in a minute sucker pad.

► **A Collared lizard**
(*Crotaphytus collaris*)
suns itself on a rock.
Lizards are cold-
blooded animals, and
sunbathing helps them
to regulate their body
temperature.

colour and patterns to match their background. At the same time, they keep a careful watch for an unwary insect with their eyes, each of which can be swivel-led independently in its socket. When close enough to its prey, a chameleon shoots out its enormous sticky tongue and quickly reels it in again, with the insect caught on the tip (see page 99).

Escape tactics
Most lizards stay out of the way of attackers by hiding in dark narrow places. When sunbathing in the open during warm weather, they are very sensitive to sudden movements and can vanish in an instant, making only the faintest rustle. If they are caught they have a marvellous safety device – they can shed their tails at will. Most lizards' tails are fragile and break off if pulled hard. The

attacker is often left holding a still wriggling tail, while its prey escapes. The lizard normally grows a replacement tail, which is slightly smaller but works as well as the old one.

Some lizards protect themselves by pretending to be dead until the attacker goes away. Others are more aggressive. The Australian frilled lizard (*Chlamydosaurus kingii*) holds its ground, startling its attacker by turning on it with mouth open and the skin of its neck spread out into an angry ruff.

If the legendary dragon lives it must be the huge lizard of the island of Komodo, in Indonesia. The Komodo dragon (*Varanus komodoensis*, see page 177) feeds on pigs, small deer, and even water buffalo. There are stories of it killing people who have strayed too close.

Snakes

Snakes' extraordinary bodies set them apart from most other animals. Without legs, shoulders, eyelids or obvious ears, they are streamlined in motion, whether swimming, or slithering along the ground or through the branches of trees. There are nearly 2400 species of snake in the world, ranging in size from 10 cm long to monster species 12 metres long.

Hunters and killers

Snakes are meat-eaters and have various ways of catching and killing their prey. Some simply crush small animals in their jaws. Pythons and boas, on the other hand, wrap themselves around their victim and suffocate it. The Reticulated python (*Python reticulatus*) of South-East Asia is one of the species that can even kill large mammals such as pigs and deer in this way.

Some snakes use poison, called venom, to help them subdue and kill their prey. When this type of snake bites, it plunges its sharp fangs into its victim's body. The venom then flows from the fangs into the animal's bloodstream. Smaller animals are killed, but larger species are only paralyzed. Around 300 snake species are venomous, but only some of them are deadly to humans.

Snakes are helped when hunt-

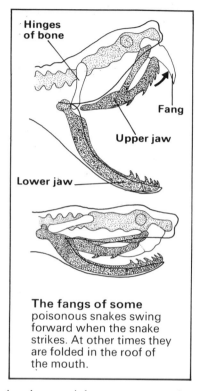

The fangs of some poisonous snakes swing forward when the snake strikes. At other times they are folded in the roof of the mouth.

ing by special sense organs. In addition to sight and hearing, and sensitivity to vibration, they can smell and taste the environment with their tongues. As it constantly flicks in and out, a snake's tongue collects chemicals from the air or ground. These are interpreted by a special organ in the mouth. Snakes can trail their prey using this method.

Some snakes have even more amazing sense organs which en-

able them to track their prey in total darkness. Most boas and pythons, and many vipers, have holes in their heads which lead to heat-detecting cells. These cells allow the snakes to follow the body heat given out by their prey – a small mammal hiding in its burrow at night, for example.

► The Amethystine python (*Morelia amethystina*) is Australia's largest snake.

▲ A Green tree python (*Chondropython viridis*), with its powerful body in coils.

Crocodiles and relatives

The members of the order Crocodylia are the largest surviving reptiles on Earth. They are related to those animal giants the dinosaurs, which became extinct 65 million years ago.

The order is divided into three families – crocodiles (family Crocodylidae), alligators and caimans (family Alligatoridae), and the Gharial (family Gavialidae). They all have tough leathery skin and enormous jaws lined with sharp teeth for tearing the flesh of their prey. Crocodiles and alligators eat a range of different animals, including mammals, birds, fish, and other reptiles. The Gharial (*Gavialis gangeticus*) feeds only on fish.

Catching a meal

When hunting large mammals such as antelopes, a crocodile

▲ **An Estuarine crocodile** (*Crocodylus porosus*) shows its sharp teeth and powerful tail. This species is the largest living reptile.

will submerge itself in the water of a river or lake, lying quietly until the animals come down to take a drink. The crocodile then lunges forward to grab its prey, holding it beneath the water surface until it drowns.

Baby crocodiles eat invertebrates such as insects and molluscs, and they spend a lot of their time searching among riverside plants for a meal. When they reach about 1 metre in length, the young crocodiles are big enough to hunt in the water. They start by catching fish and graduate to birds and mammals as they grow and become more skilled at catching and killing.

Bringing up baby

Like most reptiles, crocodiles and alligators lay eggs. Afterwards, they cover the eggs with a mound of earth and vegetation. As the vegetation rots, it gives out heat which keeps the eggs warm as they develop. At a certain stage in the egg's development, the mound temperature determines the sex of the baby reptile. A temperature below 30°C produces females, while males hatch out if it rises above 34°C. Why this happens is still something of a mystery, even to biologists.

Crocodile parents guard their nests and look after their babies very carefully. If danger threatens, the parent will pick up its young and keep them safe in its mouth and throat. When the coast is clear, the parent spits the babies out again.

Crocodile

Alligator

Gharial

▲ **The three crocodylian** families differ mainly in the arrangement of their teeth and jaws. Alligators and crocodiles are very similar, but when a crocodile closes its jaw, a tooth still shows on either side of its mouth.

REPTILE RECORDS

Largest crocodile – the Estuarine crocodile (*Crocodylus porosus*) often reaches 6 metres, but can be as long as 7.5 metres. It is found in southern Asia and northern Australia.

Largest lizard – Indonesia's Komodo dragon (*Varanus komodoensis*) can be 3 metres long and weigh 136 kg.

Largest turtle – the Leatherback (*Dermochelys coriacea*) is 2.7 metres long and can weigh 820 kg!

Longest snake – probably the Reticulated python (*Python reticulatus*) of South-East Asia, which reaches 10 metres. The Anaconda (*Eunectes murinus*) can also be this long.

Most dangerous snake – the Black mamba (*Dendroaspis polylepsis*) of Africa and the Taipan (*Oxyuranus scutellatus*) of northern Australia probably have the most deadly venom. The Indian cobra (*Naja naja*) is less poisonous but more dangerous, killing thousands of people with its bite each year.

Birds

Birds are the only vertebrates, apart from bats, that can fly. They have developed two ways of doing this – they either glide on outstretched wings or they flap their wings up and down. Sometimes they use a combination of both methods, but most birds push themselves along through the air by flapping their wings. Gliding species, which include large birds such as eagles, have to flap their wings when taking off, of course.

▼ **Some beautifully coloured** birds – Toco toucan (*Rhamphastos toco*) left; Red bird of paradise (*Paradisaea rubra*) below; Common pheasants (*Phasianus colchicus*) bottom.

A bird's wing is actually a modified arm. It is extremely light, partly because the bones are rather thin, and it can be neatly folded back next to the body when not in use. The feathers grow out from the skin, like the hairs of mammals. Long flight feathers grow from the hand and forearm, while smaller contour feathers grow from the top of the wing. The feathers also make a smooth surface, which lets the air flow easily over the wing in flight.

Birds are warm-blooded – like mammals, but unlike fish, amphibians and reptiles. Because of this, birds and mammals can keep themselves warm and therefore active even when the air is colder than their bodies are. The various mammal species keep their bodies at between 30°C and 39°C – the normal body temperature of humans, for example, is 37°C. However, birds have a constant body temperature of about 40°C. It is only at this higher temperature that their powerful flight muscles are able to work at peak efficiency.

Flightless birds

Not all birds can fly, and flightless species include the largest of all birds, the Ostrich (*Struthio camelus*) of Africa and the Emu (*Dromaius novaehollandiae*) of Australia (see page 112). These species are too heavy to fly and their wings are small in comparison to their body size. Like the related flightless cassowaries (family Casuariidae) of north Australia and New Guinea, and rheas (family Rheidae) of South America, Ostriches and Emus have long muscular legs. All these birds can run quickly as well as defending themselves by kicking.

New Zealand is home to several flightless birds. There are three species of kiwi (family Apterygidae), all about the size of a hen and with tiny wings which lie hidden under fur-like feathers. They are nocturnal, spending the day hiding in burrows or among tree roots and emerging at night to sniff out insects or fruit and leaves to eat. New Zealand's Kakapo (*Strigops habroptilus*) is a flightless parrot, which hides under roots and rocks by day and comes out at night to feed.

There are over 8800 species of bird, ranging in size from the Ostrich, which stands 2.5 metres tall and can weigh up to 150 kg, to tiny hummingbirds which can weigh as little as 2 grams. Different species inhabit all corners of the world, from the heat of the tropics right into the cold of the polar regions.

Class Aves
- Body covered by feathers
- Lay large eggs with shells
- Two legs, with scaly feet
- Front limbs are wings
- Beak, but no teeth
- Breathe through lungs
- Warm-blooded

▲ **Kiwis are hen-**sized flightless birds from New Zealand.

◄ **The Emu** (*Dromaius novaehollandiae*) of Australia can't fly, but it can run very quickly on its powerful hind legs.

▼ **Penguins are** flightless birds which spend much of their lives in the sea. They breed on land.

Table 6 – Bird groups

There are around 8800 bird species, grouped in 28 orders.

Rank	Common name	Species known
Order Struthioniformes	Ostrich	1
Order Rheiformes	Rheas	2
Order Casuariiformes	Emu, cassowaries	4
Order Apterygiformes	Kiwis	3
Order Tinamiformes	Tinamous	49
Order Sphenisciformes	Penguins	16
Order Gaviiformes	Loons/Divers	4
Order Podicipediformes	Grebes	20
Order Procellariiformes	Albatrosses, shearwaters, petrels & relatives	92
Order Pelecaniformes	Pelicans, gannets, cormorants & relatives	57
Order Ciconiiformes	Herons, storks, ibises & relatives	114
Order Anseriformes	Waterfowl	152
Order Falconiformes	Birds of prey	286
Order Galliformes	Game birds	263
Order Gruiformes	Cranes, rails, bustards & relatives	191
Order Charadriiformes	Shorebirds, gulls, terns, auks & relatives	317
Order Pterochidiformes	Sandgrouse	16
Order Columbiformes	Pigeons & doves	300
Order Psittaciformes	Parrots, lories, cockatoos & relatives	328
Order Cuculiformes	Cuckoos, turacos & relatives	150
Order Strigiformes	Owls	133
Order Caprimulgiformes	Nightjars, frogmouths & relatives	98
Order Apodiformes	Swifts, hummingbirds	389
Order Trogoniformes	Trogons	37
Order Coliiformes	Mousebirds	6
Order Coraciiformes	Kingfishers, bee-eaters, hoopoes & relatives	193
Order Piciformes	Woodpeckers, toucans, barbets & relatives	378
Order Passeriformes	Passerines/Perching birds	5206

Making a meal

Although their bodies are all basically similar, birds show huge variety in their feeding methods, with certain species having special features that allow them to feed in particular ways. The main differences are in the shape of the beak and the feet.

Kingfishers (family Alcedinidae) and other birds that feed on fish have long sharp beaks and streamlined bodies. They launch themselves like living missiles, plunging into the water of a river or lake and catching their prey in their scissor-like beaks. The Anhinga (*Anhinga anhinga*) even uses its thin sharp beak to spear live fish underwater.

The Osprey (*Pandion haliaetus*) is a fish-eating hawk. It also plunges into the water, but feet first, as it catches fish in its large rough claws.

Many birds are meat-eaters and hunt and kill other birds and small mammals for food. Owls (order Strigiformes) are nocturnal hunters and have large eyes to help their night-time vision. They also have very good hearing and can locate a rustling mouse with great accuracy, from well above the ground. They fly slowly and silently and surprise their prey by pouncing, their sharp claws spread out in attack.

Other bird species are adapted to feed on invertebrates. Treecreepers (family Certhiidae) have thin, slightly curved beaks which they use to prise insects out from underneath tree bark. Woodpeckers (family Picidae) use their sharp dagger-like beaks to dig into the wood in search of grubs.

The flamingo (family Phoenicopteridae) has a unique feeding method. It places its large beak upside down in the water, allows it to fill, then strains edible invertebrates from the water through special filters on its tongue.

BIRD RECORDS

Largest – male Ostriches (*Struthio camelus*) can reach 2.5 metres in height and weigh around 155 kg.

Heaviest flying bird – the Great bustard (*Otis tarda*) can weigh as much as 18 kg.

Largest wingspan – the Wandering albatross (*Diomedea exulans*) measures more than 3.5 metres between wingtips.

Smallest – the Vervain hummingbird (*Mellisuga minima*) of Jamaica grows to only 5.8 cm and weighs just 2 grams.

Fastest – the swifts (family Apodidae) fly the fastest, with a species of spine-tailed swift, *Chaetura gigantea* of eastern Asia, achieving about 145 km/h. Peregrines (*Falco peregrinus*), however, can reach 400 km/h in a falling stoop!

► **Hummingbirds beat their** wings very quickly as they hover feeding in flowers. This Long-tailed hermit hummingbird (*Phaethornis superciliosus*, from French Guiana) is sipping nectar from a Hibiscus flower.

▼ **A European kingfisher** (*Alcedo atthis*) surfaces from a dive, a small fish held firmly in its beak. Most birds' feathers are kept waterproof by a coating of oil, which is applied by the bird during preening.

Plant food

Seeds are a good source of energy, and parrots (family Psittacidae) are one of a number of bird groups whose beaks are powerful enough to crack open tough seed cases. Some of the larger seed-eaters, such as pheasants and other game birds (order Galliformes), swallow seeds whole and then grind them up in a special muscular part of their gut, called the gizzard.

The hummingbirds (family Trochilidae), the sunbirds (family Nectariniidae) and the honey-eaters (family Meliphagidae) all have thin curved beaks and long tongues, which they poke down inside flowers to extract the sweet nectar. The shape of each hummingbird species' beak actually matches the shape of the flowers on which it feeds!

Perching birds

◄ **The Common jay** (*Garrulus glandarius*) lives in woodland in Europe and Asia.

▼ **Waxwings take** their name from the red tips to their flight feathers. They live in forests in northern Asia and North America.

Just under 60 per cent of all birds belong to the order Passeriformes, the perching birds. They include some of the most beautiful species, as well as the finest songbirds. The feet of perching birds have three toes facing forwards and one facing backwards, which gives ideal grip in trees.

Many common garden birds are perching birds, including the thrushes (family Turdidae), finches (families Fringillidae and Ploceidae), and crows and jays (family Corvidae). Members of the family Corvidae are frequent visitors to farmland, where some people regard them as pests to crops. Actually, crows and jays feed mainly on invertebrates in the soil, such as insect larvae.

Birds of paradise (family Paradisaeidae) are among the most beautiful and colourful of perching birds (see the photograph on page 110). As in many bird species, however, the females are rather drab. Female birds of paradise have dull brown plumage, but the feathers of the males are bright blue, red and yellow, depending on the species. These special feathers are used in courtship displays to attract the females during the breeding season. Birds of paradise live in mountain forests of New Guinea and north-eastern Australia.

Nest-builders

As their name suggests, weaverbirds (family Ploceidae) are skilful builders. Some species construct complicated nests, weaving them from grasses and twigs. The Social weaverbird (*Philetairus socius*) of southern Africa breeds in colonies of up to 300 pairs Underneath a woven dome-shaped roof, in a tall tree, each pair builds its own hanging nest chamber. The result is a huge communal nest, 4–5 metres across!

Even more remarkable are the bowerbirds (family Ptilonorhynchidae) of New Guinea and northern Australia. Their twig nests are simple, but the courtship areas, or bowers, built by the males are very unusual. Male bowerbirds are great collectors and they gather all sorts of objects – shells, flowers, moss and berries – to decorate their bowers. Some species even paint the walls of their bowers, using plant pigments mixed with saliva and a piece of bark as a brush.

▲ A Black-headed weaverbird (*Ploceus cucullatus*) building its hanging nest.

▼ A male Satin bowerbird (*Ptilonorhynchus violaceus*) at the entrance to his bower.

Birds of prey

These meat-eaters are classified in the order Falconiformes. They range in size from the huge vultures and condors, whose wingspan reaches 3 metres, to the tiny falconets, which are only 16.5 cm long from head to tail.

All birds of prey have strong hooked beaks and large feet with long sharp claws called talons. They also have big eyes and very acute vision. All of these features help birds of prey to spot and catch their food – this includes other birds as well as small mammals such as mice.

Vultures and condors (families Accipitridae and Cathartidae) are carnivores that feed on dead animals but do not kill for themselves. They have bare, featherless skin on their heads and necks which makes it easier for them to feed inside the dead animal's carcass, or body.

Eagles (family Accipitridae) are a majestic sight as they soar high above open country, hunting small mammals such as rabbits and hares. The Golden eagle (*Aquila chrysaetos*) is found in mountainous country in Europe, Asia and North America. Golden eagles build huge nests, called eyries, on rocky crags. They add to the nest each season, and old eyries are sometimes several metres thick.

Falcons (family Falconidae) are speedy flyers with pointed streamlined wings and long tails. Some, like the Peregrine (*Falco peregrinus*), are able to catch and kill other fast-flying birds in mid-air. The Peregrine's smaller relative, the Hobby (*Falco subbuteo*), can even kill such agile birds as swallows and swifts.

▲ The Bald eagle (*Haliaetus leucocephalus*) is the United States' national bird. It is named because, from a distance, its white head makes it look bald. It feeds mainly on fish, which it tears apart with its large powerful beak. Although it is still common along the coast of Alaska, it is rare elsewhere.

► **A Golden eagle**
(*Aquila chrysaetos*)
with its young in its
eyrie, or nest. Eagles are
fierce hunters and have
keen eyesight and
sharp beaks.

▼ **The Peregrine**
falcon (*Falco
peregrinus*) feeds on
other birds, chasing
and catching them in
flight. Peregrines are
found on every
continent, except
Antarctica.

Water birds

Many birds are adapted for life in or on the water. They often have either webbed or lobed feet to help them swim, and beaks that are large enough to catch and hold the fish and other water animals they eat.

Members of the order Anseriformes (waterfowl) include about 150 species of ducks, geese and swans. They all have short legs with webbed feet and are good swimmers. Geese and swans have long necks and can reach down into shallow water for their food.

The swans are the largest of the waterfowl. Most are graceful, pure white birds which breed in early summer in the Arctic regions and fly south in large flocks in the autumn. One species, however, the Black swan (*Cygnus atratus*) of Australia, is entirely black, with a bright red bill.

Some birds specialize in feeding at the water's edge – the margins of rivers, lakes and ponds, as well as the seashore. Called waders, they include plovers (family Charadriidae) and sandpipers (family Scolopacidae). They have long legs on which they wade about in shallow water hunting for food. Many waders have long straight bills which they can poke into soft mud to reach crustaceans and worms hiding in it.

▼ **The colourful male** Mandarin duck (*Aix galericulata*).

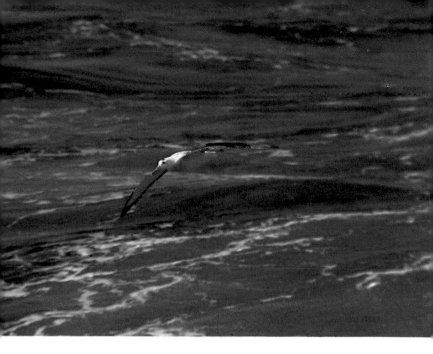

Seabirds

Even the open seas are not without bird life. Penguins (order Sphenisciformes) cannot fly, but they are excellent swimmers. Their wings are paddles with which they propel themselves through the water at speeds up to 40 km/h. Penguins have a thick layer of feathers, whose surface is smooth and waterproof, and they glide easily through the water without getting wet.

Albatrosses (family Diomedeidae) and shearwaters (family Procellariidae) are also adapted for ocean life. They are not really swimmers, though. They have long narrow wings and spend most of their lives gliding over the sea, coming ashore only to nest and lay eggs.

▲ **The Wandering albatross** (*Diomedea exulans*) is the largest bird of the open ocean. It has a wingspan of 3.5 metres.

▼ **The Oystercatcher** (*Haematopus ostralegus*) is a wader and feeds at the water's edge. It uses its bill to prise open the shells of bivalves.

121

Mammals

To many people, mammals are the creatures they mean when they talk about 'animals'. In fact, mammals only account for a tiny 0.3 per cent of all animal species!

The feature that is unique to mammals is that the females feed their young on milk. This energy-rich food is produced by the body of the mother in special organs called mammary glands. The positioning of the mammary glands varies between species. Human mammary glands are called breasts and they are positioned on the chest, for example. In sheep, cows, deer and horses, the glands are between the back legs. In cats, dogs and pigs, they are in two rows along either side of the belly.

Mammals are warm-blooded and most have hair or fur covering their bodies to help keep them warm. Species that live in water often have thick layers of blubber, or fat, under the skin to keep out the cold, or thick waterproof fur.

Mammal groups

There are three major groups within the mammals class – the monotremes, the marsupials and the placental mammals. The divisions are based on differences in the way the animals reproduce and in the development of their young. Although monotremes feed their young on milk, they are the only mammals that lay eggs.

The females of most marsupial species have a special pouch called a marsupium, which contains their mammary glands. Their babies are born blind and at a very early stage in their development, and they live in the pouch until fully grown.

More than 90 per cent of mammals are placental. With these animals, most of the baby's development takes place inside the mother's body. The baby receives its nourishment from the mother's bloodstream via an organ called the placenta.

◄ **Mammals are the only** animals that feed their young on milk produced in the mother's body. Here, a Rhesus macaque (*Macaca mulatta*) suckles a baby at her breast. These macaques live in northern India and Pakistan. They are a type of monkey and they are classified in the order Primates, family Cercopithecidae.

Class Mammalia
- Body with fur or hair
- Young fed on mother's milk
- Jaws, usually with teeth
- Usually four-limbed
- Breathe through lungs
- Warm-blooded
- Mostly terrestrial

Table 7 – Mammals

There are about 4150 species of mammal, classified into 21 different orders. Table 8, on page 165, details the order Primates.

Rank	Common name	Species known
ORDER MONOTREMATA	**Monotremes**	**3**
Family Tachyglossidae	Echidnas	2
Family Ornithorynchidae	Platypus	1
ORDER MARSUPIALIA	**Marsupials**	**c. 270**
Family Didelphiidae	American opossums	75
Family Microbiotheriidae	Monito del monte	1
Family Coenolestidae	Shrew/Rat opossums	7
Family Dasyuridae	Quolls, dunnarts, marsupial mice & relatives	53
Family Myrmecobiidae	Numbat	1
Family Thylacinidae	Thylacine/Tasmanian wolf	1
Family Notoryctidae	Marsupial mole	1
Family Peramelidae	Bandicoots	17
Family Thylacomyidae	Rabbit-eared bandicoots/ Bilbies	2
Family Phalangeridae	Phalangers	14
Family Burramyidae	Pygmy possums	7
Family Pseudocheiridae	Ringtail possums	16
Family Petauridae	Gliders	7
Family Macropodidae	Kangaroos, wallabies	50
Family Potoroidae	Rat kangaroos	10
Family Phascolarctidae	Koala	1
Family Vombatidae	Wombats	3
Family Tarsipedidae	Honey possum	1
ORDER INSECTIVORA	**Insectivores**	**c. 345**
Family Tenrecidae	Tenrecs, otter shrews	33
Family Solenodontidae	Solenodons	2
Family Erinaceidae	Hedgehogs, moonrats	17
Family Soricidae	Shrews	246
Family Chrysochloridae	Golden moles	18
Family Talpidae	Moles, desmans	29
ORDER CHIROPTERA	**Bats**	**c. 960**
Suborder Megachiroptera (1 family)	Flying foxes	175

ORDER CHIROPTERA cont.		
Suborder Microchiroptera	(all other bats)	781
Family Rhinopomatidae	Mouse-tailed bats	3
Family Craseonycteridae	Hog-nosed bat	1
Family Emballoneuridae	Sheath-tailed bats	50
Family Noctilionidae	Bulldog bats	2
Family Nycteridae	Slit-faced bats	12
Family Megadermatidae	False vampire bats	5
Family Rhinolophidae	Horseshoe bats	70
Family Hipposideridae	Leaf-nosed bats	61
Family Phyllostomatidae	Spear-nosed bats	140
Family Desmodontidae	Vampire bats	3
Family Mormoopidae	Ghost-faced bats	8
Family Vespertilionidae	Vesper bats	320
Family Natalidae	Funnel-eared bats	8
Family Furipteridae	Thumbless bats	2
Family Thyropteridae	Disk-winged bats	2
Family Myzopodidae	Sucker-footed bat	1
Family Mystacinidae	Short-tailed bats	2
Family Molossidae	Free-tailed bats	91
ORDER EDENTATA	**Edentates**	**29**
Family Myrmecophagidae	Anteaters	4
Family Megalonychidae	Sloths (two-toed)	2
Family Bradypodidae	Sloths (three-toed)	3
Family Dasypodidae	Armadillos	20
ORDER LAGOMORPHA	**Lagomorphs**	**58**
Family Ochotonidae	Pikas	14
Family Leporidae	Rabbits, hares	44
ORDER MACROSCELIDEA	**Elephant shrews**	**15**
ORDER CARNIVORA	**Carnivores**	c. **230**
Family Felidae	Cats	35
Family Canidae	Dogs & relatives	35
Family Ursidae	Bears	7
Family Viverridae	Civets, mongooses & relatives	66

◄ **Genets** (*Genetta genetta*) belong to the family Viverridae.

Phylum	Common name	Species known
ORDER CARNIVORA cont.		
Family Procyonidae	Raccoons, pandas & relatives	17
Family Mustelidae	Weasels & relatives	67
Family Hyaenidae	Hyaenas	4
ORDER CETACEA	**Whales & dolphins**	**76**
Suborder Odontoceti	Toothed whales	66
Family Platanistidae	River dolphins	*5*
Family Delphinidae	Dolphins	*32*
Family Phocoenidae	Porpoises	*6*
Family Monodontidae	White whales	*2*
Family Physeteridae	Sperm whales	*3*
Family Ziphiidae	Beaked whales	*18*
Suborder Mysticeti	Baleen whales	10
Family Eschrichtidae	Grey whale	*1*
Family Balaenopteridae	Rorquals	*6*
Family Balaenidae	Right whales	*3*
ORDER PINNIPEDIA	**Seals & sea-lions**	**34**
Family Otariidae	Eared seals	14
Family Odobenidae	Walrus	1
Family Phocidae	True seals	19
ORDER SIRENIA (2 families)	**Dugong & manatees**	**4**
ORDER PHOLIDOTA (1 family)	**Pangolins**	**7**
ORDER SCANDENTIA (1 family)	**Tree shrews**	**18**
ORDER DERMOPTERA (1 family)	**Flying lemurs/Colugos**	**2**
ORDER RODENTIA	**Rodents**	**c. 1700**
Family Castoridae	Beavers	2
Family Aplodontidae	Mountain beaver	1
Family Sciuridae	Squirrels, marmots & relatives	267
Family Geomyidae	Pocket gophers	34
Family Anomaluridae	Scaly-tailed squirrels	7
Family Heteromyidae	Pocket mice	65
Family Pedetidae	Springhare	1
Family Muridae	Rats, mice & relatives	1082
Family Gliridae	Dormice	10
Family Seleviniidae	Desert dormouse	1
Family Zapodidae	Jumping & birch mice	14
Family Dipodidae	Jerboas	31
Family Erethizontidae	New World porcupines	10

ORDER RODENTIA cont.		
Family Caviidae	Cavies	14
Family Hydrochoeridae	Capybara	1
Family Myocastoridae	Coypu	1
Family Capromyidae	Hutias	13
Family Dinomyidae	Pacarana	1
Family Agoutidae	Pacas	2
Family Dasyproctidae	Agoutis, acouchis	13
Family Abrocomidae	Chinchilla rats	2
Family Echimyidae	Spiny rats	55
Family Chinchillidae	Chinchillas, viscachas	6
Family Octodontidae	Degus/Octodonts	8
Family Ctenomyidae	Tuco-tucos	33
Family Thryonomyidae	Cane rats	2
Family Petromyidae	African rock rat	1
Family Hystricidae	Old World porcupines	11
Family Ctenodactylidae	Gundis	5
Family Bathyergidae	African mole-rats	9
ORDER ARTIODACTYLA	**Even-toed ungulates**	**186**
Family Suidae	Pigs	9
Family Tayassuidae	Peccaries	3
Family Hippopotamidae	Hippopotamuses	2
Family Camelidae	Camels & relatives	6
Family Tragulidae	Chevrotains	4
Family Moschidae	Musk deer	3
Family Cervidae	Deer	36
Family Giraffidae	Giraffe, okapi	2
Family Bovidae*	Bovids	121
Subfamily Antilocaprinae	Pronghorn antelope	*1*
Subfamily Bovinae	Wild cattle	*23*
Subfamily Cephalophinae	Duikers	*17*
Subfamily Hippotraginae	Grazing antelopes	*24*
Subfamily Antilopinae	Gazelles, dwarf antelopes	*30*
Subfamily Caprinae	Sheep, goats & relatives	*26*
ORDER PERISSODACTYLA	**Odd-toed ungulates**	**16**
Family Equidae	Horses, asses, zebras	7
Family Tapiridae	Tapirs	4
Family Rhinocerotidae	Rhinoceroses	5
ORDER PROBOSCIDEA (1 family)	**Elephants**	**2**
ORDER HYRACOIDEA (1 family)	**Hyraxes**	**11**
ORDER TUBULIDENTATA (1 family)	**Aardvark**	**1**

*The members of the cattle, sheep and antelope family, the Bovidae, are so varied that six subfamilies are recognized.

Monotremes

Although they are classed as an order, Monotremata, there are only three monotreme species alive today. Two are echidnas, or spiny anteaters. The Short-beaked echidna (*Tachyglossus aculeatus*) is common throughout Australia and is also found in New Guinea, but the other species, the Long-beaked echidna (*Zaglossus bruijni*), lives only in the New Guinea highlands.

Echidnas have fur and spines. They tuck their legs and head under their bodies if disturbed, and their sharp spines protect them from attack. They have a thin snout, with a tiny mouth at the tip, and they use their long sticky tongue to catch their diet of worms, ants and termites.

The third monotreme is the Platypus (*Ornithorhynchus anatinus*), the most bizarre of mammals. Its combination of webbed feet and a duck-like beak with a long furry body makes it seem more like an invention than a real

▲ **Platypuses (*Ornithorynchus anatinus*)** have webbed feet and rather duck-like beaks.

animal. In fact, when the first specimen was sent to Britain from Australia in 1798, many scientists thought it was a fake and that someone was playing a practical joke!

The male Platypus is the only mammal with a poisonous sting. Its venom is contained in a pointed spur behind the ankle of each of its back legs. The sting can be very painful to humans and can kill small mammals. Echidnas have these spurs too, but they do not contain poison.

Platypuses live in tunnels in the banks of streams and rivers, and find the invertebrates on which they feed by grubbing about in the mud and gravel of the riverbed. The Platypus' beak is very sensitive to movement and helps it to track and catch its food underwater.

▲ **A Short-beaked echidna** (*Tachyglossus aculeatus*) shuffles along on its strong clawed feet. Echidnas' long sensitive noses help them to hunt worms to eat.

Order Monotremata

- Lay eggs
- Adults toothless
- Males have poison spurs
- Only found in Australia and New Guinea

Marsupials

◀ **A female Eastern** grey kangaroo (*Macropus giganteus*), with a joey in her pouch. Baby kangaroos are little more than 2.5 · cm long when they are born. They make their way quickly to the mother's pouch, remaining there for about six months while they grow and develop.

Of the 270 or so species in the order Marsupialia, around 65 per cent are found in Australia and New Guinea, while the remainder inhabit the Americas. Marsupials are thought to have originated in South America and to have spread to Australia about 60 million years ago, when these continents were joined to Antarctica as a single landmass.

Kangaroos and wallabies (family Macropodidae) are probably the best-known marsupials. They are herbivores and the main difference between them is size – wallabies are generally smaller than kangaroos.

Their huge muscular back legs make kangaroos and wallabies good jumpers, and they can bound along at speed using their tails to steady themselves. Baby kangaroos are called joeys. They ride safely inside the mother's pouch for several months, often with just their head poking out – sometimes just a leg shows!

The biggest marsupials are kangaroos – the Eastern grey (*Macropus giganteus*) and the Red (*Macropus rufus*) can be 2.7 metres from head to tail-tip and weigh 90 kg.

Possums and opossums

Australia and New Guinea are home to the marsupials known as possums. Australia's most familiar species is the Common brushtail possum (*Trichosurus vulpecula*), which lives in towns

▶ **Koalas (*Phascolarctos cinereus*)** are slow-moving Australian marsupials, which feed almost entirely on the leaves of certain types of Eucalyptus tree. They are agile climbers and spend most of their time in trees, rarely coming down to ground level.

◀ **The Virginia** opossum (*Didelphis virginiana*) spends much of its life on the ground in wooded country. It will climb trees to escape danger, but sometimes it pretends to be dead – thus the expression 'playing possum'.

as well as in the bush. It looks like a large squirrel, with huge eyes and a long fluffy tail.

The Americas have two groups of marsupial – the American opossums (family Didelphidae) and the shrew or rat opossums (family Caenolestidae). Confusingly, they are sometimes called possums for short. One species, the Virginia opossum (*Didelphis virginiana*), is common in the United States. This opossum is expanding its range, in fact, and is now found right up over the border into southern Canada.

Not all marsupials are herbivores. There are a number of small species which resemble mice and rats, and which mostly feed on small invertebrates. Some are fiercely carnivorous and catch and eat quite large animals, including lizards. There are also some small marsupials which don't have pouches. These include the mouse opossums (genus *Marmosa*).

Insectivores

As their name suggests, animals in the order Insectivora are adapted for a diet of insects. Most are nocturnal and have sensitive noses and a good sense of smell, which helps them to track and catch insects to eat.

The biggest insectivore group is the shrews (family Soricidae). Because they are small and shy, and most active after dusk, shrews are not often seen, but you may hear their high-pitched squeaks in the hedgerows.

Shrews have sharp teeth and can inflict painful bites. They eat a range of invertebrates, besides insects, and include worms and spiders in their diet. Some, like the American short-tailed shrew (*Blarina brevicauda*), even eat larger animals such as fish and frogs. This species has poisonous saliva which it injects when biting its prey, to help kill it.

Moles and hedgehogs

Moles (family Talpidae) are tunnellers and are rarely seen because they spend most of their lives underground. Usually we only know that moles are about by the molehills they throw up on the surface of the ground.

Moles dig with their shovel-shaped front feet. They make a series of connected burrows and live off the insects and worms they stumble into while moving around the network of passages. Few species of mole are actually blind, but moles' eyes are very small and their vision is probably limited to telling the difference between light and dark.

Another group of insectivores, the hedgehogs (family Erinaceidae), are common in Europe. They are covered in sharp spines and protect their soft bellies by rolling up into a tight ball. This habit is very effective against predators, as it prevents them from getting a grip. Unfortunately, it is no protection against road traffic, and many hedgehogs are killed by cars and other motor vehicles.

► **With its long** pointed nose and short legs, the Common shrew (*Sorex araneus*) of Europe is a typical insectivore. It has small eyes, but well-developed senses of hearing and smell.

▲ Moles (*Talpa europaea*) are tunnel diggers and have powerful front feet and long claws.

▼ **Their sharp spines protect** hedgehogs (*Erinaceus europaeus*) from their enemies.

Order Insectivora

- Insect-eaters
- Small and active, with short limbs
- Small ears and eyes
- Long narrow noses

Bats

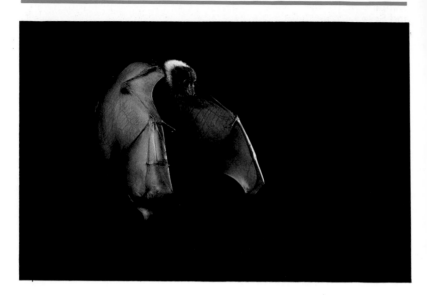

Bats are the only vertebrates, apart from birds, that can fly. Some mammals can glide, but bats stay airborne for long periods of time by flapping their wings just like birds do. A bat's wing is quite different from that of a bird, however. It is formed out of a thin layer of skin, which is supported by the long finger bones of the hand – rather like a tent on its frame. The skin stretches to the base of the bat's feet and across to its tail.

The bat order, Chiroptera, has two suborders. The flying foxes (suborder Megachiroptera) are large bats with good eyesight. They are active in the day and feed on fruit, nectar and pollen.

Creatures of the night

Most bats are nocturnal and belong to the other suborder, Microchiroptera. The majority are insect-eaters, but some catch fish. A few – the false vampires (family Megadermatidae) – even catch birds and small mammals.

Although vampire bats (family Desmodontidae) feed on blood, they are not dangerous to humans. Only one of the three vampire bat species, the Common vampire (*Desmodus rotundus*), attacks mammals. It crawls up to sleeping cattle, horses or pigs and bites them with its razor-sharp teeth. It does not suck the blood, but simply licks it up as it oozes out of the wound.

▶ **A Common**
vampire bat (*Desmodus rotundus*) at rest, hanging from a twig. Vampires live in Central and South America and feed on the blood of birds and mammals. They are small animals, around 6 to 9 cm long.

◀ **This Indian fruit**
bat (*Pteropus giganteus*) is one of the largest species of flying fox – its wingspan can be 2 metres. Bats' wings are extensions of the skin of their bellies and backs. The bones of their four fingers make a framework, supporting the wing, but the thumb sticks out and can be used for holding food.

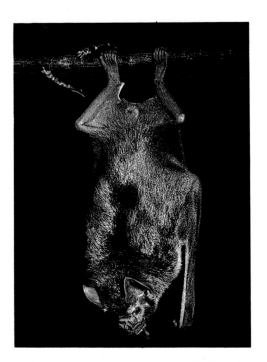

The other two species, the White-winged vampire (*Diaemus youngi*) and the Hairy-legged vampire (*Diphylla ecaudata*), feed mainly on birds' blood. All three bats are found only in Central and South America.

Nocturnal bats have a special feature which enables them to fly perfectly well even in pitch darkness, when it is impossible to see. These bats send out a continuous stream of very high-pitched sounds as they fly. They find their way by listening to the echoes made as the sounds bounce off objects. This is called echolocation. With it bats can even find insects such as moths and catch them in flight.

Many bats are small, like the insectivores to which some biologists believe they are related. The smallest mammal of all is a bat – Kitti's hog-nosed bat (*Craseonycteris thonglongyae*) of Thailand is only about 3 cm from head to tail and weighs 1.5 grams. The biggest bats are the flying foxes, some of which have a wingspan of 2 metres and weigh as much as 1.5 kg.

Order Chiroptera
- Only mammals that fly
- Front limbs are wings
- Very sensitive ears; echolocation used in flight
- Mostly nocturnal

Toothless mammals

Of the three animal families in this order, Edentata, only the anteaters are really toothless. The others, the sloths and the armadillos, have a very simple form of rootless teeth.

Anteaters (family Myrmecophagidae) feed on ants, of course, but some species also take termites and insect larvae. The four species of anteater are all found in Central and South America. The biggest, the Giant anteater (*Myrmecophaga tridactyla*), is more than 2 metres long when it is fully grown.

When an anteater finds an ants' nest, it rips into it with its sharp curved claws. To feed, the anteater flicks its long tongue in and out of the nest. Its tongue has tiny spines and is covered with sticky saliva. Insects that stick to it are drawn back with the tongue right into the ant-eater's mouth.

Walking tanks

Armadillos (family Dasypodidae) look like anteaters with armour plating. This 'armour' is actually bony plates, coated with horn, which grow in the skin. Like the other members of this order, armadillos are rather slow-moving and they would be easy prey for carnivores such as foxes were it not for their special protective shield. When threatened, an armadillo pulls in its legs to protect its soft vulnerable belly. Some species can even roll up completely into a ball.

▼ **The Giant anteater**
(*Myrmecophaga tridactyla*) walks on the knuckles of its front legs, turning its long sharp claws inwards.

▶ **A sloth can turn** its head through 270 degrees and hold it almost upright, even when upside down. It spends much of its life hanging from branches, clinging on with its long curved claws. Although they belong to the order Edentata, the toothless mammals, sloths have simple teeth in their cheeks. They feed on leaves and fruit.

Armadillos do not have front teeth but rely on small peg-like teeth in their cheeks for grinding up their food. They eat fruit and small vertebrates, as well as termites and ants. Most species are found only in South and Central America, but the Common or Nine-banded armadillo (*Dasypus novemcinctus*) has spread up into the United States.

Hanging loose
Sloths (families Megalonychidae and Bradypodidae) are also slow-moving animals, as their common name indicates. They live in the South American rainforests and there are five species –

two of these have two toes, and three have three toes.

Sloths spend most of the time upside down in trees, clinging on with their curved claws. Their shaggy fur is often a greenish colour because of the algae growing in it. Even their digestion is slow and it can take a month for a meal to pass through a sloth's body. They have simple grinding teeth, but they lack front teeth.

Order Edentata
- No teeth; or simple rootless teeth
- Most have long claws
- Slow-moving

Rodents

The word rodent comes from the Latin *rodere*, meaning to gnaw, and animals in this order have special teeth for grinding and gnawing at a whole range of food, including nuts and even wood. Rodents' teeth are constantly being worn-down through use, and to cope with this the front ones keep on growing throughout the animal's life.

Rodents have long whiskers on their noses, and sometimes above the eyes as well. These are sensitive to touch and help rodents to judge the size of gaps when moving about in narrow places, especially at night when they hunt.

Most rodents are small – rats, mice, voles and dormice, for example – and some are kept as pets, including guineapigs and hamsters. All pet hamsters are thought to be descended from one pregnant Golden hamster (*Mesocricetus auratus*) which was caught in the Middle East in the 1930s. Young from this litter were taken to Britain and the United States and the pet animals were bred from them.

Like all rodents, the Black rat (*Rattus rattus*) has strong front teeth for gnawing food. To make up for the wearing effect of their diet, rodents' teeth grow constantly, like fingernails.

◀ **The Common** dormouse (*Muscardinus avellanarius*) of Europe mainly lives in trees and bushes, feeding on buds, soft fruit and nuts.

▼ **Capybaras** (*Hydrochoerus hydrochaeris*) always live near water.

The largest rodent species is the Capybara (*Hydrochoerus hydrochaeris*) of South America. It looks like a huge guineapig and can grow as tall as 60 cm at the shoulder and weigh 66 kg.

Capybaras graze in small groups near rivers and lakes. They are very good swimmers and take to the water when disturbed. Their eyes, ears and nostrils are high on their heads, and this allows them to float almost unseen in the water.

Capybaras are harmless herbivores, but unfortunately for them they are good to eat, while their skin makes good quality leather. In Venezuela, they are even farmed like cattle, on special ranches.

Order Rodentia
- Most are small and active, with short limbs
- Sharp front teeth
- Long sensitive whiskers

Rodent acrobats

Most squirrels (family Sciuridae) are more at home in the trees than on the ground. Once in a tree they move so fast that they can vanish from sight within seconds. Their sharp claws dig into the bark to help them climb – sometimes they even manage this upside down!

Several species are called flying squirrels (genera *Petaurista* and *Pteromys*, for example). They can glide from tree to tree on the parachute-like pieces of skin that stretch between their front and back legs. Using this method, a flying squirrel can escape its enemies by launching itself into the air.

Not all squirrels live in trees,

▲ **A flying squirrel launches** itself into the air, to glide on 'wings' of tightly stretched skin.

however. Marmots (genus *Marmota*) and prairie dogs (*genus Cynomys*), for example, live in underground burrows.

Rodent builders

With a head-to-tail length of about 1.5 metres, beavers (family Castoridae) are very large rodents. They spend most of their lives in and under the water. There are two species – the European beaver (*Castor fiber*) and the North American beaver (*Castor canadensis*).

Both beavers have an amazing ability to fell trees by gnawing through the trunks. They use the timber to build their homes, called lodges, and to construct dams across rivers.

Young beavers are called kits, and they are born in the safety of the lodge in late spring. They are looked after and fed by their parents for a period of months, although they are well adapted to life in water and can swim very soon after birth.

A beaver swims by kicking its webbed back feet. Sometimes it flaps its huge flattened tail as well, but this is normally used like a rudder to change direction while swimming. The tail is also used to make alarm signals. If a beaver is disturbed, it will sometimes slap its tail hard on the surface of the water. The loud noise acts as a warning to the other beavers in the area.

◄ ▼ **Beavers live in** burrows in river banks, or build lodges like this in the water. The central chamber is always above water, to keep it dry. Underwater entrances stop most enemies from entering.

Rabbits and hares

These animals are grouped in the order Lagomorpha. They have strong front teeth for gnawing, rather like those of rodents, and they can chew seeds and thick roots as well as graze on grasses and herbs. Unlike rodents, though, rabbits and hares have large ears and eyes. Since their eyes are positioned at the sides of their heads, they can keep a lookout for danger in front and behind them without moving any part of their bodies.

Rabbits and hares use their big back legs for hopping and running, often achieving high speeds over short distances. Many species live and feed in open country and rely on their speed to escape from predators such as birds of prey, and foxes and stoats. Large hares can reach 80 km/h when running flat out.

▼ **A Black-tailed jack rabbit** (*Lepus californicus*) pricks its ears, alert for signs of danger.

▲ Hares have long hind legs and can run very fast, but they rely on twisting and leaping to escape their enemies. This species is the European hare (*Lepus europaeus*).

▶ When a rabbit bounds away from danger, the sight of its bobbing white tail warns other rabbits to do the same. This is the European rabbit (*Oryctolagus cuniculus*).

Hares (genus *Lepus*) are mostly larger than rabbits, with longer ears, and they can run faster because they have longer hind legs. Species that live in areas which get a lot of snow in winter change colour in the autumn from brown to white. This acts as camouflage, helping them to blend in with their background and escape predators.

Hares rear their young in nests called forms, which they build on the ground. Baby hares, called leverets, are born with all their fur and with their eyes open. They are strong enough to run within a few days.

Despite their name, the jack rabbits of North America are actually types of hare. They are closely related to other hares, such as the European (*Lepus europaeus*), the Snowshoe (*Lepus americanus*) and the Arctic (*Lepus timidus*) hares.

Rabbit species include the European rabbit *Oryctolagus cuniculus* and the cottontails of North America (genus *Sylvilagus*). Most live underground, in tunnels which they dig by scrabbling at the earth with their sharp front paws and kicking out the loose soil with their big hind feet.

Rabbits retreat into their burrows when danger threatens. Their young, known as kittens, are born in underground nesting chambers. Unlike leverets, kittens are born naked.

Order Lagomorpha
- Large ears
- Sideways-facing eyes
- Slit-like nostrils
- Very short tail

Carnivores

The word carnivore means 'meat-eater', and most of the members of this group feed by catching and eating other animals. Dogs, cats, bears, raccoons, weasels, mongooses and hyaenas are all carnivores. In all, there are about 230 species, found in many different habitats throughout the world – from the wolves and Arctic foxes of the icy north, to the tigers of India.

To help them rip up flesh, carnivores have special sharp teeth called carnassials. These have jagged edges and can be clamped hard into the meat to tear it up into bite-sized chunks. Most carnivores, especially the dogs and cats, also have large sharp canine teeth near the front of the mouth.

Weasels and relatives

These animals are grouped in the family Mustelidae. Weasels themselves (genus *Mustela*) are rather short-legged, slender creatures. They feed on mice, voles and other small mammals, and sometimes birds. One North American species, the Fisher (*Martes pennanti*), has a liking for porcupines. It deals with their bristling spines by flipping the porcupine over and attacking its soft underbelly.

Otters (genera *Lutra*, *Enhydra* and others) are like large weasels that have taken to an aquatic lifestyle. They feed mostly on fish and are brilliant and acrobatic swimmers, spending most of their lives in the water. Their hind feet are webbed to help with swimming, and their fur is very tightly packed and waterproof.

Like the other members of the weasel family, badgers (genus *Meles* and others) are shy animals which are most active at dusk or during the night. They are rarely seen because of this, even though they are quite common in meadows and woodland.

◀ **Stoats (*Mustela erminea*)** have brown summer coats but grow white fur in winter. This winter coat is called ermine and it is prized by fur traders. In North America *Mustela erminea* are known as Short-tailed weasels.

► **A Cape clawless otter** (*Aonyx capensis*) eating fish. Otters are very shy and difficult to spot in the wild.

▼ **Badgers have short** powerful legs and strong claws for digging. Their homes are large burrows called sets, which they line with bracken and other vegetation. Badgers eat roots and fruit, as well as invertebrates and small vertebrates such as mice.

Cats

The members of the family Felidae are superb hunters. They stalk their prey quietly, creeping slowly close to the ground until they are near enough to make a sudden dash to catch it with their sharp claws. They then hold the animal down with their claws while they kill it, usually by biting. Cats are able to retract, or pull in, their claws when they don't want to use them.

Most of the 35 cat species belong to the genus *Felis* and are known as the small cats. They include the Lynx (*Felis lynx*) and the Ocelot (*Felis pardalis*), as well as the hundreds of domestic cat breeds, all of which are thought to be descendants of the Wild cat (*Felis silvestris*).

The big cats

There are seven species of big cat – the Tiger (*Panthera tigris*), Lion (*Panthera leo*), Jaguar (*Panthera onca*), Leopard (*Panthera pardus*), Snow (*Panthera uncia*) and Clouded (*Neofelis nebulosa*) leopards, and the Cheetah (*Acionyx jubatus*).

The big cats are very similar to the small cats in their general body shape and behaviour, although the big cats are much more dangerous, of course, and can kill and eat large animals.

Other differences include the fact that small cats purr, big cats roar. Small cats also tuck their front paws in when resting, whereas big cats stretch their feet out in front of them.

Lions are the big hunters of the African plains. They live in groups called prides, each one with about 15 members. The lionesses do nearly all of the hunting, and they also help each other to feed the cubs in the pride. The larger males seem to spend a lot of the time dozing!

The Jaguar is mostly found in the tropical forests of Central and South America. It has beautiful orange-coloured fur, blotched with black. Occasionally, as with the leopards, completely black specimens are found. Jaguars climb trees, but they are also good swimmers.

◄ Some members of the cat family. The black cat in the centre is a type of Leopard (*Panthera pardus*), often called a Black panther.

1: Domestic cat (*Felis silvestris catus*)
2: Wild cat (*Felis silvestris*)
3: Caracal (*Felis caracal*)
4: Lynx (*Felis lynx*)
5: Tiger (*Panthera tigris*)
6: Snow leopard (*Panthera uncia*)
7: Lion (*Panthera leo*)

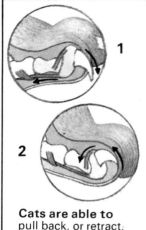

Cats are able to pull back, or retract, their claws (2).

147

Dogs

The dog family, the Canidae, includes wolves, jackals and foxes, as well as the familiar domestic pet.

Dogs are built for running in the open, usually in packs. Their claws are needed to help them run. They are blunter than cats' claws and cannot be retracted. Dogs rely more on biting than on using their claws to capture prey.

The Grey or Timber wolf (*Canis lupus*) is the largest wild species of dog. It lives in forested and mountainous areas of North America, Europe and Asia, and is even found north into the Arctic. Sometimes Grey wolves hunt in packs, sometimes alone. Their diet is varied and includes deer, as well as small mammals and even berries. Despite their reputation, they are not dangerous to people.

Coyotes (*Canis latrans*) are like small wolves. They are quite common in the United States and western Canada, and they are

▼ **The hundreds of different** breeds of Domestic dog (*Canis familiaris*) are all thought to be descended from the Grey wolf. The dogs below are used as working dogs, but they are often kept as pets, too.

Collie

Rottweiler

French sheepdogs

Belgian sheepdog

Kelpie (Australian sheepdog)

Corgis

Old English sheepdog

148

▲ **A Grey wolf** (*Canis lupus*) patrols a forest border. Wolves hunt by day and sleep at night, hidden under fallen trees, among rocks, or in holes they dig in the ground.

▶ **The Bat-eared fox** (*Otocyon megalotis*) lives in dry grasslands in Africa.

spreading north and eastwards, sometimes breeding with wolves and Domestic dogs. Besides insects and fruit, they eat small mammals such as mice and rabbits – even, sometimes, large ones like deer and sheep.

Foxes are small, rather dainty members of the dog family. Over 20 species have been identified and more than half are classified in the genus *Vulpes*. They all have large ears and big bushy tails. They eat almost anything, from mice, insects, worms and birds, to fruit and household rubbish. The Red fox (*Vulpes vulpes*) is common in Europe and North America, and has even taken to living in towns.

Perhaps the strangest fox is the Bat-eared fox (*Otocyon megalotis*). Its enormous ears help it listen out for its insect prey.

► **Like all bears, the Brown** bear (*Ursus arctos*) only rears up on its hind legs if it wants to get a good look at something or to scare an intruder. Usually it ambles along on all fours.

Bears

Although they are classed as carnivores, bears eat a range of food, including fruit, roots, fish and small mammals.

There are only seven species in the bear family, the Ursidae. The Brown or Grizzly bear (*Ursus arctos*) and the American black bear (*Ursus americanus*) are both large species, but the biggest is the Polar bear (*Ursus maritimus*) – males can grow to 3 metres and sometimes weigh 800 kg.

Polar bears live in the Arctic region, where their yellowish white fur blends in well with the background of ice and snow. This helps to camouflage them while they approach their prey. They are the most carnivorous of all the bears and eat mostly seals.

Polar bears have very dense fur and a thick layer of insulating fat to keep out the intense cold of the Arctic.

The Brown bear is found right across Asia and in Canada and the north-western United States, where it is known as the Grizzly bear. It is now very rare in most of Europe. Grizzlies include a lot of fish in their diet. They collect at rivers when salmon come up to lay their eggs, scooping the fish out of the shallow water as they swim past.

The smaller bears are the Asian black bear (*Selenarctos thibetanus*), the Sloth bear (*Melursus ursinus*), the Spectacled bear (*Tremarctos ornatus*) and the Sun bear (*Helarctos malayanus*). The Spectacled bear is South America's only bear. The other three species inhabit South-East Asia.

Pandas

Despite their appearance, pandas are not bears. They belong instead to the family Procyonidae, which includes the raccoons. There are only two species of panda – the Red panda and the Giant panda.

The Red panda (*Ailurus fulgens*) is the smaller of the two species. It lives in forests in parts of northern India, Nepal and Burma, and in southern China. It has chestnut-coloured fur and a rather fox-like shape, as well as a long tail.

The Giant panda (*Ailuropoda melanoleuca*) is familiar as the symbol of conservation adopted by the World Wide Fund for Nature (formerly, the World Wildlife Fund). Its diet is very specialized and it feeds almost exclusively on bamboo stems. It is only found in certain mountain bamboo forests in southern China, where it is carefully protected – today there are probably fewer than 1000 Giant pandas remaining in the wild.

▼ **The bear-like Giant panda** (*Ailuropoda melanoleuca*) is one of the world's rarest mammals. Its natural habitat is bamboo forests in the mountains of western China. This region is remote, and little is known about pandas' behaviour in the wild.

Marine mammals

There are three orders of mammals that live in the sea, but they are not closely related.

The order Sirenia embraces just four species – the Dugong or Sea-cow (*Dugong dugon*) and three types of manatee (genus *Trichechus*). All are herbivores and rather rare. Their bodies are large – 3 to 4 metres long – and streamlined, but very fat, with a thick layer of blubber. They don't have hind limbs and their front ones are rather paddle-like.

▲ **Grey seals (*Halichoerus grypus*)** live off rocky coasts in north-western Europe. They don't have ear flaps and are therefore classified in the family Phocidae, the true seals.

Order Pinnipedia

- Front and hind limbs are flippers
- Short stocky neck
- Earflaps small, or missing altogether
- Marine, but breed on land

Sirenians are peaceful creatures which swim about slowly in warm tropical seas and river estuaries, eating water plants. Some people think it was these gentle animals that gave rise to stories about mermaids.

Seals and sea-lions

The second order of marine mammals, Pinnipedia, contains 34 species in all. Although these sleek and graceful animals live at sea, they have to come ashore to breed, either on ice or at deserted rocky coasts. They are flesh-eaters. Depending on the species, their diet ranges from fish and crustaceans to birds and even other seals.

There are two groups of seal – eared seals (family Otariidae) and true seals (family Phocidae). As their name suggests, seals in the first group have ears. These stick out from the side of the head as small flaps. Eared seals use their front flippers to swim,

and their back flippers are adapted to help them shuffle along on land. The family contains the sea-lions and fur seals.

True seals don't have ear flaps. Instead, they have small holes in their head which lead directly to the inner ear. Their back feet are simple flippers and cannot be used for walking. They swim by bending their sleek bodies from side to side in the water.

The Walrus (*Odobenus rosmarus*) is in a group of its own – family Odobenidae. Its tusks are actually huge curved upper teeth, which stick down on either side of its mouth. Like elephants' tusks, they are a source of ivory. Both males and females have tusks, and they use them for grubbing in the seabed for food and for smashing breathing holes in the ice. Walruses also use their tusks rather like icepicks to help them climb out of the water. Rival males fight each other with their tusks, as well.

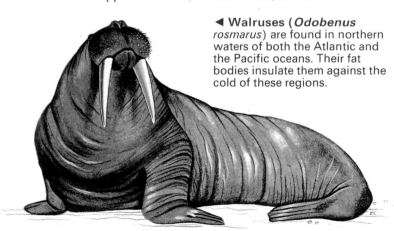

◀ **Walruses (*Odobenus rosmarus*)** are found in northern waters of both the Atlantic and the Pacific oceans. Their fat bodies insulate them against the cold of these regions.

153

Whales and dolphins

These animals are grouped in the order Cetacea. They are completely marine and even breed in the sea.

Like sirenians but unlike other mammals, neither whales nor dolphins have any form of back legs. Most species are shaped very like large fish and even have a fin on their backs. Indeed, until about 200 years ago, biologists actually thought that they were a type of fish. However, whales and dolphins are warm-blooded, like other mammals, and they feed their young on milk. They also have lungs and breathe air.

Dolphins and porpoises are grouped in the suborder Odontoceti, the toothed whales. They feed mostly on fish and squid, using their sharp teeth to catch and tear up their prey. The group includes the Killer whale (*Orcinus orca*) which rarely threatens people, despite its name.

Most of the bigger whales are classified in the suborder Mysticeti, the baleen whales. These whales have strainers called baleen plates in their mouths, to filter food such as krill and small fish from mouthfuls of water as they swim along. The Blue (*Balaenoptera musculus*) and Humpback (*Megaptera novaeangliae*) are baleen whales.

Tuning in

Dolphins, porpoises and other toothed whales have a special method of finding their way about underwater and of identifying their prey – they make high-pitched sounds and listen to the echoes these sounds make as they bounce off objects. This is rather similar to the way bats find their way about in the dark, and both navigation methods are called echolocation.

Some whale species communicate with each other underwater by making a wide range of sounds. These sounds have been recorded using underwater microphones and they sound quite song-like, if rather eerie. Some are pitched too high or too low for human ears to pick up, however.

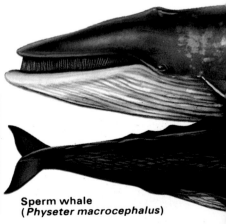

Sperm whale
(*Physeter macrocephalus*)

Order Cetacea

- Front limbs are flippers; no hind limbs
- Most have single back fin
- Fish-like tail
- Nostrils on top of head
- Aquatic; nearly all marine

▲ **Bottlenose** dolphins (*Tursiops truncatus*) are found in warm coastal waters worldwide.

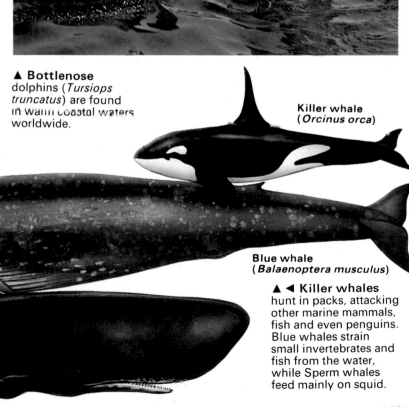

Killer whale (*Orcinus orca*)

Blue whale (*Balaenoptera musculus*)

▲ ◄ **Killer whales** hunt in packs, attacking other marine mammals, fish and even penguins. Blue whales strain small invertebrates and fish from the water, while Sperm whales feed mainly on squid.

155

Hoofed mammals

There are two main types of hoofed mammal, or ungulate – the even-toed (order Artiodactyla) and the odd-toed (order Perissodactyla). In even-toed species, the hoof is formed from two or four strengthened toes, while in the odd-toed species one or three toes are involved.

Ungulates' hooves are hard and horny and they protect the feet when the animals are moving fast, especially over rough ground. Most of the members of this group are good at running in open country.

▲ **Hoofed mammals rely on** speed to escape predators. These Gemsbok (*Oryx gazella*) are large African antelopes which live in dry, semi-desert regions.

All hoofed mammals are herbivores, feeding mostly on herbs, grasses, leaves, twigs and fruit. They graze in herds, sticking close together for protection against the carnivores that prey on them. Hoofed mammals have good eyesight and a keen sense of smell. They can also hear well and are constantly alert and on the lookout for danger.

Chewing the cud

The cells of plants contain large amounts of a substance called cellulose, which is very difficult to digest. Hoofed mammals have various adaptations which help them feed on plants. Most species' teeth are flat-topped and work by grinding down the plant cells to release their contents. This grinding action is possible because a hoofed mammal's bottom jaw moves from side to side, as well as up and down. You can see this movement very clearly if you watch a cow feeding.

Deer, antelopes, giraffes, cattle, sheep, goats and camels are all ruminants. They have a special stomach with four chambers instead of the usual one, and their method of eating is known as 'chewing the cud'. When these animals swallow, the food goes into a chamber called the rumen. Here it is fermented by bacteria, which break down the plant cell walls. The fermented food, the cud, is then passed back into the mouth, where it is chewed again. Finally, it is passed to the three other parts of the stomach for digestion. This slow method of eating extracts as much goodness as possible from plant food.

▶ Giraffes (*Giraffa camelopardalis*) use their flexible sensitive lips to gather leaves and twigs from tall trees. A Giraffe's horns are covered with skin, and this gives its head a strange knobbly look.

157

Even-toed ungulates

This is the biggest of the two ungulate groups, with over 185 species. The order Artiodactyla includes all the ruminants as well as pigs and hippos.

Many even-toed species have horns. Some have short horns – a few species of goat, for example, and the smaller species of antelope such as gazelles, as well as giraffes. Other ungulates have very large horns, which are either twisted into a spiral, as in the American bighorn sheep (*Ovis canadensis*), or gracefully curved, like those of the Sable antelope (*Hippotragus niger*).

Instead of horns, deer have antlers. These are rather like horns, but whereas horns are kept by an animal for life, antlers are shed every year and have to be regrown each season. Usually, only males grow antlers, but both male and female Reindeer or Caribou (*Rangifer tarandus*) have large antlers. The heavy antlers of a male Moose (*Alces alces*) may be 2 metres across.

▲ **Caribou (*Rangifer tarandus*)** live in small bands of 5 to 100, or in herds numbering up to 3000. In Europe, they are called Reindeer.

◄ **The Sable** antelope (*Hippotragus niger*) lives in eastern and central Africa, but is now rather rare.

Amphibious ungulate

The Hippopotamus (*Hippopotamus amphibius*) is the most unlikely member of the even-toed ungulates – it looks nothing like the graceful, athletic deer and antelopes!

Hippos can lose a lot of body water as sweat through the skin, and during the heat of the day they spend their time wallowing in mud or swimming and resting in water. At night, they leave for feeding grounds where they browse on leaves and grasses.

Male hippos sometimes fight and can give each other nasty wounds with their sharp tusks. These are enlarged lower canine teeth, and they can be as long as 50 cm in adult males.

Orders Artiodactyla and Perissodactyla

- Walk on toes strengthened as hooves
- Herbivores, with flattened teeth for grinding food
- Some have horns or antlers

► **A Hippo's tusks** are enlarged canine teeth. Hippos spend most of the day in water, floating almost submerged, with only their ears, eyes and nose above the surface. They emerge at night to feed on grasses, uprooting them with their tough lips.

Odd-toed ungulates

This order consists of the families Rhinocerotidae (rhinos), Tapiridae (tapirs) and Equidae (horses, asses and zebras). There are only 16 species in all.

Rhinos are sturdy animals, with their tough skin and heavy, muscular bodies. Both males and females have long pointed 'horns' on their heads, on top of the nose. These aren't made of bone, but are actually very tightly packed hair.

Rhino 'horns' are valued as the material for dagger handles and as medicine with supposed magical properties. They are the main reason why rhinos are hunted and killed by people. Such hunting is illegal, but it continues and has made some species rather rare.

Tapirs live in the tropical forests of South America and the

▲ **White rhinoceroses**
(*Diceros bicornis*) can be 4 metres long and weigh 2300 kg.

Malaysian peninsula. They look rather pig-like, but they have an unusual, flexible upper lip, which looks rather like a tiny trunk. Using its lip, a tapir can grasp twigs and leaves to eat as it trots about in the forest.

There are three species of zebra, all of them inhabiting plains and grasslands in eastern and south-west Africa. They live in groups, sometimes of as many as 200, and share their habitat with antelopes and other herbivores. With their stripes and colour, zebras stand out from their background and are easy for their enemies to spot. Their main predators are large carnivores such as lions, hyaenas and hunting dogs.

► **Tapirs use their** flexible snouts to gather plants to eat. This is Baird's tapir (*Tapirus bairdi*) of Central and South America.

▼ **No one knows** why zebras are striped, but it may help them to follow and stay close to each other in herds, thereby gaining some protection from their enemies.

Elephants and oddities

◀ **The Aardvark**
(*Orycteropus afer*)
feeds on termites and
ants, using its long
powerful claws to rip
their nests open, then
licking the insects out
with its sticky tongue.

Although they look so dissimilar, elephants, hyraxes and the Aardvark are all thought to be related. The connection is not close, though, and the animals are classified in different orders. They share some features with the ungulates. Their feet are rather hoof-like, for example, especially those of elephants.

The Aardvark (*Orycteropus afer*) is so odd that it has an order all to itself, the Tubulidentata. It lives in scrub and grassland in south and central Africa, but is seldom seen because it is nocturnal. Aardvarks feed on ants and termites – to help them do this they have long snouts and, like anteaters, long sticky tongues.

There are two species of elephant, grouped in the order Proboscidea – the word is from the Greek for 'nose'. The Asian or Indian elephant (*Elephas maximus*) has been domesticated in India and its strength has been used in war as well as in the timber industry. This is also the species you'll see performing tricks in circuses. In the wild the Indian elephant lives in forests, where it feeds on leaves, grasses and fruit. Elephants are herbivores, despite their size!

The African elephant (*Loxodonta africana*) is the biggest living species of land animal. Large adult bulls, or males, weigh around 6 tonnes and are often over 3 metres tall. African elephants live south of the Sahara, in bush, forest, or even semi-desert country. They move about in small groups, feeding on grasses, twigs and bark.

The price of teeth

Elephant tusks are very large teeth, which emerge when the animal is about two years old and continue to grow throughout its life. They are used only occasionally for fighting and fending off attackers. Males and females of both elephant species have tusks, but they rarely show in female Indian elephants.

Like all mammals' teeth, tusks contain dentine, or ivory. Unfortunately, elephants' tusks are large enough to provide a lot of this valuable material – the tusks of old bull elephants sometimes grow to be over 3 metres long. African elephants are killed in enormous numbers by poachers, who get a high price for the ivory, and because of this slaughter the survival of this magnificent animal is in doubt.

Hyraxes

There are 11 species of this unusual animal, grouped in the order Hyracoidea. Hyraxes are all small and rather rodent-like – they look like a cross between a squirrel and a guineapig. They have rubbery pads on their feet and short nails, however, not the sharp claws typical of rodents.

Hyraxes live mostly in the dry regions of south and central Africa, and in the Middle East.

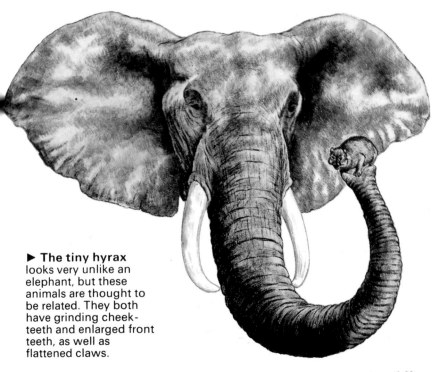

▶ **The tiny hyrax** looks very unlike an elephant, but these animals are thought to be related. They both have grinding cheek-teeth and enlarged front teeth, as well as flattened claws.

Primates

The primate groups are generally thought to contain the most advanced of the animals. Hence the order name, given because it holds the prime, or highest, position in the animal kingdom. Most primates have large brains and a well-developed ability to learn about their surroundings. Monkeys and apes even communicate with each other using a type of language, and some species have acquired the ability to use simple tools.

Humans are primates, and all the members of the order Primates have human-like hands and feet, with a thumb or a big toe which can be moved independently of the other digits to grip objects such as tree branches or food. Primates tend to have fleshy pads on their fingers and

▼ **Chimpanzees** (*Pan troglodytes*) can grip objects firmly and will use twigs as tools to take insects from their nests. They also use stones to crack nuts – or as missiles to throw at their enemies!

toes, with flat nails instead of claws. This is another adaptation that allows primates to hold objects firmly – long curved claws would get in the way.

Primates have various ways of moving around their different habitats. Most walk on all fours and jump well, using their long back legs. Others are adapted for living high in the trees and use their tail rather like a fifth limb. Some species, such as the gibbons and chimpanzees, can even walk upright on their hind legs for short distances.

Lower and higher primates
There are two primate suborders. The animals in the suborder Prosimii are known as the lower primates. They have longer noses and smaller brains than animals in the other suborder, and a much less human appearance. Their eyes face sideways slightly and are large for night vision, as many species are nocturnal.

The suborder Anthropoidea contains the higher primates. These animals have flattish faces, with eyes that face forwards. Most have short, upturned noses and small ears.

Order Primates
- Well-developed hand, with separate thumb
- Large brain
- Large, forward-facing eyes with binocular vision

Table 8 – Primate groups

Rank	Common name	Species known
SUBORDER PROSIMII	**Lower primates**	**36**
Family Lemuridae	Lemurs	10
Family Cheirogaleidae	Dwarf & mouse lemurs	7
Family Indriidae	Indri, sifakas	5
Family Daubentoniidae	Aye-aye	1
Family Lorisidae	Bushbabies, potto, lorises	10
Family Tarsiidae	Tarsiers	3
SUBORDER ANTHROPOIDEA	**Higher primates**	**147**
Family Cebidae	Howler monkeys & relatives	30
Family Callitrichidae	Marmosets, tamarins	21
Family Cercopithecidae	Old World monkeys	82
Family Hylobatidae	Lesser apes	9
Family Pongidae	Great apes	4
Family Hominidae	Humans	1

Lower primates

Of the 36 species in the suborder Prosimii, over 20 are lemurs. These unusual animals are only found on the island of Madagascar, off the south-east coast of Africa. The word lemur means 'ghost' and these creatures can seem very mysterious, especially at night as they move about in the treetops, sometimes calling with strange howls or grunts.

Lemurs live in forest trees and eat mostly fruit, seeds, flowers and leaves. Not all of them are nocturnal. In general the smaller species, such as the dwarf and mouse lemurs (family Cheirogaleidae), are active at night, and the larger ones (families Lemuridae and Indriidae) in the day.

All lemurs have large eyes and ears, and rather pointed noses. They are beautiful creatures, with soft fur and long woolly tails – the beautiful black and white tail of the Ring-tailed lemur (*Lemur catta*) is longer even than its body. One species, however, has just a short stump of a tail. This is the largest of the lemurs, the Indri (*Indri indri*), which grows to about 70 cm.

The body of the smallest lemur, the Lesser mouse lemur (*Microcebus murinus*), is just over 12 cm long. This animal is also the smallest primate.

Bushbabies (genus *Galago*) are nocturnal, like the small lemurs. They inhabit forested regions of eastern Africa, where they feed at

▶ **Two Lesser** bushbabies (*Galago senegalensis*) gaze nervously out from a tree stump. Their large eyes help these nocturnal primates to hunt in the dark.

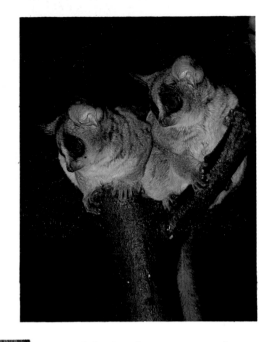

◀ **A Ring-tailed** lemur (*Lemur catta*) leaps from a tree, its long tail stretched out to balance it.

▼ **Tarsiers live in** trees and move about by leaping from branch to branch. Their huge eyes and sensitive ears help them to track insects and small lizards to eat.

night in the trees, mostly on insects. Bushbabies have big eyes and ears and can follow insects just by listening to them.

The three species of tarsier (family Tarsiidae) are only found on the Indonesian islands of Borneo, Sumatra and Sulawesi, and in parts of the Philippines.

Tarsiers have huge eyes – each one weighs more than the individual animal's whole brain – and they can swivel their heads almost in a full circle to see.

A tarsier hunts by sitting on branches close to the forest floor. When an insect or lizard passes by, the tarsier jumps on top of it, bites it with its sharp teeth, and then jumps back up into the tree branches to eat its meal.

167

Higher primates

The suborder Anthropoidea is divided into monkeys and apes. Both have flattened faces with forward-facing eyes but, unlike the apes, most monkeys have long tails.

There are three families of monkey, and most species inhabit tropical regions. Two families, the Callitrichidae (marmosets and tamarins) and the Cebidae (howler monkeys and relatives), live in Central and South America, while the third, the Cercopithecidae (Old World monkeys), is distributed throughout Africa and southern Asia.

Marmosets and tamarins

These small tree-dwelling primates behave rather like squirrels. They have long furry tails and live in small groups among the branches of forest trees, where they seek out fruit and insects to eat.

▲ **The Common marmoset** (*Callithrix jacchus*) has bushy white tufts of fur which completely cover its ears. It has the forward-facing eyes typical of higher primates.

Marmosets (genera *Callithrix* and *Cebuella*) have larger front teeth than tamarins. Marmosets use their teeth to cut holes in tree bark. Gum seeps out of the hole and this sweet nourishing food is then licked up by the animals.

Tamarins (genera *Saguinus* and *Leontopithecus*) are slightly bigger than marmosets and eat fruit and large insects. The most beautiful species is also one of the rarest. The Lion tamarin (*Leontopithecus rosalia*) has silky red-gold fur which thickens into a mane around its cheeky face (see page 176). There are probably only a few hundred left in the wild, but the Lion tamarin is being bred in captivity and may yet be saved from extinction.

Howler monkeys and relatives
This family consists of larger monkeys which are adapted superbly to life in the trees. Most species are agile climbers, with long tails that can be curled around branches and used rather like a fifth limb.

The howler monkeys (genus *Allouatta*) take their name from the loud roaring noises they produce in the early morning. Each troop makes a deafening chorus which can be heard well over a kilometre away. This howling helps rival troops to locate each other so they can avoid fighting over the food resources of their tropical forest habitat.

Old World monkeys
This is the largest of the monkey families, with about 80 species.

Guenons (genus *Cercopithecus*) are long-tailed forest monkeys which live in Africa. The Vervet monkey (*Cercopithecus aethiops*) is one of the most common species. Vervets move about in small groups in bush country and on the edge of woodland. They eat a wide range of food, including leaves and fruit, insects, rodents and birds.

Baboons (genus *Papio*) live mainly on the ground in troops of up to 200 members. They have long, dog-like muzzles with sharp teeth, and they eat a wide range of food, from seeds and grass to insects and small birds and mammals.

▼ **The Mandrill (*Papio sphinx*)** of Central Africa is the largest monkey species – males can reach 80 cm or so – and the most colourful!

◄ **A Lar gibbon**
(*Hylobates lar*) pauses in a tree. Gibbons live in the tropical rainforests of South-East Asia, and they are becoming steadily rarer as their habitat is destroyed by logging and clearing.

▶ **The Orang-utan**
(*Pongo pygmaeus*) is Asia's only great ape. It lives in thickly forested regions of Sumatra and Borneo, moving through the lower branches of trees during the day. It sleeps in the treetops, building a new nest each night. Orang-utans eat a wide range of food, but they are especially fond of fruit and will often travel long distances in search of it.

Apes

There are two families of apes. The lesser apes (family Hylobatidae) are medium-sized and spend most of their time in the trees. There are nine species and they are all gibbons which inhabit the tropical rainforests of South-East Asia.

The great apes (family Pongidae) are slower moving than the lesser apes. They climb well but spend much more time on the ground than above it. When moving along on the ground, great apes support themselves on the knuckles of their front limbs. However, they can walk for short periods on their hind legs.

Lesser apes

Gibbons are graceful animals, with very long arms which they use to swing from branch to branch high in the treetops, feeding on fruit and leaves. They keep contact with each other by very loud musical calls, which

carry long distances and echo through the forests.

Male and female gibbons pair for life and live in small family groups with two or three young. Gibbons are ready to breed when they are about six years old, and they move out of the group before starting their own families.

The Orang-utan
Although this large shy primate, *Pongo pygmaeus*, is classified as a great ape, it shares the same type of habitat as the lesser apes, the gibbons. It lives in the forests of Borneo and Sumatra, in Indonesia. Like the gibbons, the Orang-utan spends most of its time in the trees, searching for fruit. Orang-utans cannot swing in the treetops, however, and they move slowly through the lower branches.

Male Orang-utans usually live on their own, but the young stay with their mother until they are about eight years old.

Great apes

Besides the Orang-utan, there are three other species of great ape – the Chimpanzee (*Pan troglodytes*), the Pygmy chimpanzee (*Pan paniscus*) and the Gorilla (*Gorilla gorilla*). These three ape species are only found in western and central Africa, where they live in woodland and forests.

The Pygmy chimpanzee is rare and little is known about its behaviour. Chimpanzees, on the other hand, have been closely studied. They are clever animals and sometimes use tools to help them find their food, poking sticks or blades of grass into termite mounds and ants' nests to get at the insects (see the illustration on page 164). Occasionally, they break open hard-shelled fruits with a stone or a heavy stick. They eat a lot of fruit, but they will also take insects and even small mammals such as young monkeys and pigs.

Chimps live in large groups with up to 100 members, sometimes making raiding parties on neighbouring troops to steal food. They are capable of several different kinds of call, which biologists think may have particular meanings to other chimps.

Despite their size, Gorillas are harmless vegetarians and will not attack other animals, unless provoked or to defend their family from attack. They live in small groups, usually consisting of about five to ten animals, but sometimes as many as 30. Each group is made up of one adult male, with several females and young. The largest male Gorillas grow to be about 1.8 metres tall and may weigh as much as 180 kg. In the wild, Gorillas live for about 35 years.

Gorillas are normally silent, but sometimes an adult male will rear up on its legs, hooting and growling. It then beats its chest with both hands to make a hollow drumming noise, before charging forward and slapping the ground. This display may take place when two adult male Gorillas meet, but it does not usually develop into a fight.

Gorillas only inhabit small areas of tropical forest in western and central Africa. Like most of the other wild apes, their survival as a species is increasingly under threat, as more and more of their forest habitat is destroyed – either cut for timber, or cleared for agriculture or for building towns and villages. Action is urgently needed if these fascinating creatures are to survive outside zoos and animal collections.

▶ **Adult Gorillas (*Gorilla gorilla*)** have no natural enemies, apart from human hunters. Although they are the largest of the great apes, they only attack when provoked.

Animals in Danger

Mountains and oceans, tropical rainforests and temperate woodland, deserts and marshes – these are just some of the Earth's different habitats. Each has its own special climate. Each is home to a particular community of animals and plants.

Few animals can live outside their particular habitat. The destruction of South American rainforests to make grazing land for beef cattle is threatening the survival of many species, and causing others to become extinct, or die out. Even bulldozing a small wood or diverting a stream to make way for new housing has its effect on local wildlife.

Animals are in just as much danger if something interferes with the delicate balance of life in their habitat. Pollution is now a major threat. A great deal of farming land is treated with chemicals to kill weeds and wild flowers, for example, as well as insect pests to crops. This not

▼ **Cliffsides provide a safe** home for seabirds such as these Kittiwakes (*Rissa tridactyla*), as few predators can reach nests to take eggs or chicks. Kittiwakes are a type of gull.

► **The tundra is a** windswept region bordering the Arctic Ocean, and very few animals are adapted to survive conditions there. These Musk oxen, *Ovibos moschatus*, have thick shaggy fur to keep their bodies warm and can survive even fierce winter storms.

◄ **Tropical rain-** forests are home to a huge variety of animals, most of which are nocturnal and rarely seen during the daytime. Many species, especially insects, have yet to be named and classified.

only destroys insects and plants, the chemicals can build up inside the bodies of animals that feed on them, causing more deaths.

Animals are now dying out much more rapidly than ever before. Of the 8800 species of birds, for example, about 1000 are thought to be in immediate danger of extinction. Scientists believe we can expect to lose about 30 more bird species every year. For every two birds that become extinct, conservationists have calculated that we lose one mammal, six species of fish, 180 species of insects, and 70 species of plants. If animals continue to disappear at the present rate, we can probably expect to lose half of all known species within the next century.

Animals cannot survive in the wild unless their habitats are protected and conserved. This is important on a world scale nowadays – stopping the destruction of rainforests and coral reefs, for example – but it is also vital at local level. All of us can contribute by helping to protect areas that are rich in wildlife, be they a pond or a stream, a wood or even a hedgerow.

Danger file

◄ **The Lion tamarin,**
Leontopithecus rosalia, is one of the world's most endangered primates. The destruction of their tropical rainforest home and collection of these rare animals for sale as pets have combined to cause their decline in number. Only a few hundred now remain in the wild.

◄ **The Seychelles paradise** flycatcher, *Terpsiphone corvina*, is now only found on two or three islands in the Seychelles group, in the Indian Ocean. There are only about 80 birds in the main colony. This photograph shows the female bird. The male is jet black and has a longer tail.

◄ **The Southern sea otter,** *Enhydra lutris nereis*, lives in the sea off California, in the United States, but is now rather rare. It has carefully protected populations in the Monterey bay area, however. This beautiful creature often swims on its back, feeding on shellfish and using its belly as a dining table.

◄ **The Green turtle,** *Chelonia mydas*, was once found in tropical seas all over the world, from the Caribbean to the Indian Ocean. Hunting and egg stealing have now reduced its numbers drastically. In fact, all marine turtle species are now rare or threatened with extinction.

► The dog-sized **Tasmanian wolf**, *Thylacinus cynocephalus*, is the largest marsupial meat-eater. It used to be found in many parts of southern Australia and Tasmania, but has been hunted almost to extinction. There hasn't been a definite sighting since the 1930s, in Tasmania.

The Monkey-eating eagle, *Pithecophaga jefferyi*, lives in forests on the Philippine island of Mindanao, feeding on monkeys and other mammals. Fewer than 300 of this rare eagle are thought to survive.

► The **California condor**, *Gymnogyps californianus*, is a magnificent vulture which used to be found in the Sierra Nevada mountains of southern California. It has now died out in the wild, but conservationists hope to breed it in captivity and reintroduce it to its native habitat.

► The **Devil's hole pupfish**, *Cyprinodon diabilis*, is one of the world's many rare fish species. It only occurs in one spring of water in the state of Nevada, in the United States, where its population numbers between 200 and 500 fish.

► The **Komodo dragon**, *Varanus komodoensis*, reaches 3 metres in length and can weigh 140 kg. It is the world's largest lizard and it is only found on the island of Komodo and other nearby Indonesian islands. However, the population is so small that the Komodo dragon needs protection to help it survive.

Glossary

Abdomen
In invertebrate animals whose bodies are divided into three parts, the abdomen is the name given to the hind or last section of the body. The other two sections are the head and the thorax. In vertebrate animals, the abdomen is the belly area. See also Thorax.

Amphibian
Something that is equally at home on land and in water, such as frogs and other vertebrate members of the class Amphibia.

Antenna (plural antennae)
A hair-like projection from the head of certain invertebrates. Often called feelers, antennae are important as sense organs, but in some animals they have been modified to help with other tasks, such as movement.

Aquatic
Living in water. See also Marine.

Arachnid
A member of the class Arachnida (such as spiders and scorpions) which groups arthropods with two-part bodies and four pairs of legs. See also Arthropod.

Arthropod
A member of the largest animal group, the phylum Arthropoda, which includes insects, crustaceans and arachnids. All of the arthropods have jointed limbs and a hard external skeleton. See also Arachnid, Crustacean, Exoskeleton.

Binomial
The double scientific name used to classify living things. It always has a Latin form and is written in italic script – the Tiger is *Panth-*

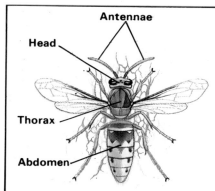

Antennae
Head
Thorax
Abdomen

All of the invertebrate animals grouped in the class Insecta have bodies that are divided into three distinct parts – head, thorax and abdomen. In many species, the body narrows to a 'waist' between the thorax and abdomen, as it does in this insect, the European hornet (*Vespa crabro*).

era tigris, for example. The first word is the genus name and the second is the species name. See also Classification.

Bivalve
A mollusc with a hinged shell.

Bone
The hard material from which the internal skeleton of most vertebrates is made. See also Cartilage, Skeleton.

Camouflage
A method of disguise. Many animals have built-in camouflage through body colour, pattern or shape, which helps them to blend in with their background and hide from predators.

Canine teeth
Many mammals, but particularly the meat-eaters, have four long pointed teeth, positioned one on each side of the top and bottom jaws. These canine teeth are used for biting and tearing.

Carapace
A hard body shield, part of the exoskeleton of some arthropods. See also Arthropod, Exoskeleton.

Carnivore
An animal that eats meat.

Cartilage
Also called gristle. A tough but flexible material, which forms the skeleton of fish in the classes Agnatha and Chondrichthyes. It is also found in the skeletons and joints of vertebrates with bony skeletons. See also Bone.

Cell
The smallest living unit. Many protozoans consist of only one cell, but the bodies of most animals contain thousands or millions of specialized cells – muscle and blood cells are two examples. See also Nucleus.

Cilia (singular cilium)
Microscopic 'hairs' which stick out from individual body cells.

Class
The third major category in the classification pyramid, after kingdom and phylum. See also Classification.

Classification
The system for cataloguing living things, by grouping together those that share similar features. There are seven major ranks – kingdom, phylum, class, order, family, genus and species.

Cold-blooded
Animals that cannot control the temperature of their bodies and have to rely on that of their environment. All invertebrates are cold-blooded, as are fish, amphibians and reptiles. See also Warm-blooded.

Colonial
Living in a group. See Colony.

Colony

A group of animals which live together. Colonial animals may live very closely and even be connected to each other in some way. For example, colonial species of coral are made up of individual animals which are joined together by thin sheets of tissue.

Many animal colonies are like extended families, however, and contain individuals who live separately but work together for the good of the group. Insects such as ants and termites live in this type of colony, as do mammals such as ground squirrels and mole-rats.

Crustacean

Crabs, lobsters, shrimps and fleas are all crustaceans and belong to the class Crustacea in the phylum Arthropoda. See also Arthropod.

Echolocation

Locating an object by measuring the time taken for sounds to travel to it, and then bounce off and return. Bats and some whales use echolocation to navigate, by sending out a stream of noise and listening to the echoes made as the sounds bounce off objects.

Exoskeleton

The hard outer skeleton which covers and protects the bodies of invertebrates such as arthropods. See also Carapace.

Family

One of the ranks in the classification pyramid, third from the bottom. The family name always ends in 'idae', for example Felidae, the cat family. See also Classification.

Fang

Special mouthparts used for injecting poison into prey. The fangs of poisonous snakes are modified teeth, for example. Spiders have claw-like fangs, while in centipedes the fangs are modified front legs.

Genus (plural genera)

The second rank up from the bottom of the classification pyramid. It always starts with a capital letter and is written in italics. See also Classification.

Gill

An organ used by aquatic animals such as fish for breathing underwater. Gills are usually feathery in structure, and lined with blood vessels. As water flows through the gills of an animal, the oxygen it carries is absorbed through the thin walls of the animal's blood vessels into the bloodstream. See also Lung.

Gland

An organ which discharges body liquids (such as sweat).

Gut

All or part of the digestive system, including the stomach.

Habitat

The environment in which an animal lives, including its climate and vegetation as well as the other animals that live there. Deserts, tropical rainforests and coral reefs are habitats, as are ponds and even hedgerows.

Herbivore

An animal that eats plants. This term is generally used to describe mammals. Other animals with this diet are usually called plant-eaters.

Hibernation

A period of deep sleep, which some animals enter when food sources are low or when the weather is very cold. During this time, which can last a period of months, the animals rarely wake and do not eat. Instead they live off stored body fat.

Host

See Parasite.

Invertebrate

An animal that does not have a backbone. Over 1.2 million invertebrate species have been classified. See also Vertebrate.

Kingdom

The highest rank in the classification pyramid. There are four kingdoms of living things – animals (Animalia), bacteria (Monera), mushrooms, toadstools and moulds (Fungi) and plants (Plantae). See also Classification.

Larva (plural larvae)

The name used to describe the young of many animals, but particularly those of invertebrates. The larvae of butterflies and moths are known as caterpillars, while those of other insect species are called grubs, or sometimes maggots.

Lung

A breathing organ which absorbs oxygen from air. All mammals have lungs, even marine mammals like whales. See also Gill.

Mammal

A member of the class Mammalia, which groups animals that feed their young on breast milk. Mammals are warm-blooded and breathe air through lungs.

Marine

Living in the sea.

Metamorphosis

This word means 'change of shape' and it is used to describe the lifecycle of animals such as insects and frogs, whose bodies go through complete changes of shape between their young and adult stages.

Mollusc

One of the invertebrate animals grouped in the phylum Mollusca. Molluscs include snails and slugs, sea shells, octopuses and squid. Most species have some form of external or internal shell. See also Bivalve.

Moulting
To cast or shed skin, hair or feathers, and replace them with new growth. Arthropods moult their exoskeletons for example.

Nerve cord
A tube of nerve cells running the length of an animal's body. A vertebrate's nerve cord is protected by its backbone.

Nervous system
The system that controls animal senses such as touch, sight and hearing.

Nocturnal
Active at night.

Nucleus
The central organ of a cell. The nucleus acts as the cell's control centre, storing the instructions for making it grow, develop and reproduce.

Nymph
The young of an insect which goes through partial (egg, nymph, adult) not complete (egg, larva, pupa, adult) metamorphosis. See also Larva, Metamorphosis.

Order
The central rank of the classification system for living things. See also Classification.

Organ
A body part with a particular function. The eye is an organ of sight, for example.

▲ **The loris (family Lorisidae)** is a nocturnal animal and has huge eyes to help it see when hunting in the dark.

Parasite
An animal that lives on or in the body of a plant or another animal (called the host), feeding on it and often causing it harm. There are also parasitic plant species.

Photosynthesis
A way of making food which employs the energy in sunlight. Green plants use photosynthesis to turn water and carbon dioxide gas from the air into sugars.

Phylum (plural phyla)
The second rank from the top of the classification pyramid. There are 33 phyla in the animal kingdom. See also Classification.

Predator
An animal that hunts and kills other animals (its prey) for food.

Prey
See Predator.

Protozoan
The simplest form of animal life, typically consisting of a single cell and its nucleus. Single-celled animals such as amoebae are grouped in the phylum Protozoa.

Radula
A rasping tongue, set with numerous tiny teeth-like pegs. It is common to most molluscs.

Reptile
A member of the class Reptilia, which groups cold-blooded vertebrates such as snakes and lizards, turtles and crocodiles.

Siphon
A tube-like organ, found particularly in molluscs. Some species use their siphons to suck in food-bearing water. Squid and cuttlefish use their siphons like water jets for rapid swimming.

Skeleton
The framework that supports and strengthens an animal's body. Vertebrate skeletons are made of bone or cartilage and include a backbone. See also Bone, Cartilage, Exoskeleton.

Species
The lowest rank in the classification pyramid. The species name is unique to each particular type of animal or plant. See also Binomial, Classification.

Tentacle
A slender projection from the body of some animals, especially invertebrates, which functions mainly as an organ of touch. Octopuses and sea-anemones have tentacles, for example.

Terrestrial
Living on land.

Thorax
In invertebrate animals whose bodies are divided into three parts (mainly insects and crustaceans), the thorax is the name given to the central section of the body. See also Abdomen.

Venom
The poisonous liquid produced by some animals to stun their prey and sometimes to kill it.

Vertebrate
An animal with a backbone. Fish, amphibians, reptiles, birds and mammals make up the subphylum Vertebrata. There are around 45,000 known species. See also Invertebrate.

Warm-blooded
The word used to describe animals that can control their body temperature. Birds and mammals are the only warm-blooded animals. Depending on species, body temperatures range between 30°C and 44°C – the normal body temperature of humans, for example, is 37°C. See also Cold-blooded.

Index

Page numbers in *italic* type refer to illustrations. Page numbers in **bold** type refer to glossary entries.

pig 158
pill millipede 63, *63*
Pinctada martensii 40
Pinnipedia (order) 126, 153
Pithecophaga jefferyi *177*
placental mammal 123, 132–72
Plaice 86, *86*, 87
Platyhelminthes (phylum) 17, 32
Platypus 128, *128*
Pleuronectes platessa 86, *86*, 87
Ploceus cucullatus *117*
plover 120
Polar bear 150
Polydesmus angustus 63
polyp (coral) 31, *31*
pond-skater 52–53, *53*
Pongo pygmaeus 171, *171*
Porcellio scaber 64
porcupine 144
Porifera (phylum) 17, 24, 25
porpoise 154
Portuguese man-o'-war 28, *29*
possum 130–31
Potato root eelworm 33
prairie dog 140
prawn 69
predator **182**
prey **183**
primate 164–72, *164–73*
Primates (order) 164–72
Pronghorn antelope 11
Prostheceraeus vittatus 33
Proteus anguinus 96
Protozoa (phylum) 17, 22–23
protozoan 9, *10*, 22, 22–23, *23*, **183**
pseudopodium 23, *23*
Pterophyllum scalare 86
Pteropus giganteus *134*
Ptilinorhynchus violaceus *117*
pupa 49
Pygmy chimpanzee 172
python 106, 107, *107*, 109
Python reticulatus 106, 109

Q

Queen conch *40*
Queensland lungfish *85*

R

rabbit 142–43, *143*
raccoon 151
radula 38, *38*, 40, **183**
Ragworm *34*
Rainbow trout *86*
Rana temporaria 90
Rangifer tarandus 158, *158–59*
rat 138, *138*
rat opossum, *see* shrew opossum
Rattus rattus 138
ray *82*, 82–83
ray-finned fish 84, 86–88, *86–89*
Red bird of paradise *110*
Red fox 149
Red kangaroo 130
Red panda 151
Reindeer 158, *158–59*
reptile 14, 98–109, *98–109*, **183**
Reptilia (class) 98–109
Reticulated python 106, 109
Rhamphastos toco *110*
rhea 111
Rhesus macaque *122*
Rhincodon typus *83*, 88
rhinoceros 160, *160*
Rhinoceros beetle *54*
Ring-tailed lemur 166, *166*
Rissa tridactyla *174*
Robber crab 64
rodent 138–41, *138–41*
Rodentia (order) 126–27, 138–41
Rotifera (phylum) 17, 36–37
Rottweiler 148
roundworm 32, 33
ruminant 157, 158

S

Sable antelope 158, *158*
Sagartia elegans 27
Sailfish 88
salamander 91, 96, 97, *97*
Salamandra salamandra 97
Salmo gairdneri *86*
sand-dollar 72
sandpiper 120
Satin bowerbird *117*
scallop 40, 41

Scaphiopus holbrookii *95*
Scolopendra gigantea 63
Scomber scombrus *86*, 87
scorpion 61, *61*
Scutigera coleoptrata 62
sea-anemone 26, *26*, 81
seabird 121, *121*
sea-biscuit 72
Sea-cow, *see* Dugong
sea-cucumber 72, *73*
seahorse *87*
seal *152*, 152–53
sea-lion 153
sea-mouse *35*
sea otter, Southern *176*
sea-squirt *74*, 75
sea-urchin 72, *72*, *73*
sea wasp 29
Selenarctos thibetanus 150
Sepia officinalis *43*
Seven-spot ladybird *54*
Seychelles paradise flycatcher *176*
shark *81*, 82–83, *83*
shearwater 121
sheep 157, 158
sheepdog *148*
shield bug *53*
shipworm 40
Short-beaked echidna 128, *129* •
Short-tailed shrew 132
Short-tailed weasel, *see* Stoat
shrew 132, *132*
shrew opossum 131
shrimp 69
siphon *39*, 43, **183**
Sirenia (order) 126, 152–53
sirenian 152–53
skate 82–83
skeleton 9, **183**
skink *101*
sloth 137, *137*
Sloth bear 150
slug 38
Small tortoiseshell butterfly *51*
Sminthillus limbatus 97
snail 38, 41
snake 98, *106*, 106–7, *107*, 109
snapping turtle 103
Snow leopard 146, *147*
Snowshoe hare 143
Social weaverbird 117

ACKNOWLEDGEMENTS

The publishers wish to thank the following for supplying photographs for this book:

Page 7 Biofotos; 8 Science Photo Library; 9 NHPA; 13 NHPA; 14 Science Photo Library; 15 Biofotos; 16 NHPA; 21 NHPA; 22 Science Photo Library; 25 Pat Morris (top), ZEFA (bottom); 27 NHPA; 28 ZEFA; 29 NHPA; 30 ZEFA; 31 NHPA; 33 Biofotos; 35 NHPA; 36 Oxford Scientific Films; 37 Oxford Scientific Films; 38 Gene Cox; 42 NHPA; 44 NHPA; 49 NHPA; 50 NHPA; 52 Oxford Scientific Films; 54 ZEFA; 55 NHPA; 56 NHPA; 57 NHPA; 58 NHPA; 60 NHPA; 61 Michael Chinery; 65 Nature Photographers; 66 Pat Morris; 67 Biofotos; 68 Biofotos (top), NHPA (centre and bottom); 70 Pat Morris; 71 NHPA; 73 NHPA; 74 Biofotos; 75 Biofotos; 77 Nature Photographers; 79 NHPA; 81 ZEFA; 82 Planet Earth Pictures; 85 NHPA; 89 NHPA; 90 NHPA; 91 NHPA; 93 Biofotos; 95 NHPA (top), Biofotos (bottom); 97 Biofotos; 98 NHPA; 99 NHPA; 101 ZEFA; 102 NHPA; 103 NHPA; 104 Pat Morris (left), NHPA (right); 105 ZEFA; 107 Pat Morris (top), NHPA (bottom); 108 NHPA; 110 Eric & David Hosking; 112 NHPA; 115 NHPA (top), ZEFA (bottom); 116 ZEFA (top), NHPA (bottom); 117 NHPA; 118 NHPA; 119 Nature Photographers (top), Eric & David Hosking (bottom); 120 Pat Morris; 121 NHPA; 122 NHPA; 129 NHPA; 130 Biofotos; 131 NHPA; 133 Biofotos; 134 NHPA; 135 NHPA; 137 Nature Photographers; 139 Swift Picture Library (top), NHPA (centre), 140 Frank Lane Picture Agency; 141 Frank Lane Picture Agency; 142 NHPA; 144 NHPA; 145 NHPA (top), Nature Photographers (bottom); 149 NHPA; 151 NHPA; 152 NHPA; 155 NHPA; 156 NHPA; 158–159 NHPA; 160 NHPA; 161 NHPA (top), Satour (bottom); 162 NHPA; 166 NHPA; 167 NHPA; 168 Frank Lane Picture Agency; 170 NHPA; 171 Frank Lane Picture Agency; 173 NHPA; 174 Biofotos; 175 Swift Picture Library (top), South American Pictures (centre); 176 NHPA; 177 Frank Lane Picture Agency (top), NHPA (centre and bottom); 182 NHPA.

Illustrations by Graham Allen (Linden Artists; p. 164); Robert and Rhoda Burns (pp. 10–11, 12, 18–19); David Webb (Linden Artists; pp. 8, 23, 24, 26, 39, 59, 163); David Wright (Middleton Artists; pp. 40, 41, 51, 53, 64).